WAYNE ROONEY

To my wife Marie – we made love our goal

IAN MACLEAY

WAYNE ROONEY

ALWAYS A BLUE

JOHN BLAKE

Published by John Blake Publishing,
3 Bramber Court, 2 Bramber Road,
London W14 9PB, England

www.johnblakebooks.com

www.facebook.com/johnblakebooks 🅵
twitter.com/jblakebooks 🆃

This edition published in 2018

ISBN: 978 1 78606 893 4

British Library Cataloguing-in-Publication Data:

A catalogue record for this book is available from the British Library.

Printed

The right of Ia   has
been asserted by   tents

Papers used by J   made
from wood gr   es
conform to

Every attempt has been made to contact the relevant copyright-holders, but
some were unobtainable. We would be grateful if the appropriate people
could contact us.

John Blake Publishing is an imprint of Bonnier Publishing
www.bonnierpublishing.com

CONTENTS

CHAPTER 1

HOMELAND

'What's past is prologue.'

THE TEMPEST – WILLIAM SHAKESPEARE

I t was a typical goal by him, a soaring leap and a powerful header that ripped into the back of the Stoke net. If you were counting there were 4,869 days between his match-winner against Mark Hughes's side and his previous goal for his beloved Everton. Rooney's goal from a neat ninja cross from Dominic Calvert-Lewin came on the stroke of half-time on a sunny August afternoon in 2017.

The Everton side lined up in a 3–4–1–2 formation read as follows:

Pickford
Keane, Williams, Jagielka
Calvert-Lewin, Gueye, Schneiderlin, Baines

WAYNE ROONEY

Klaassen
Rooney Sandro (Ramírez)

The side included the new signings Jordan Pickford, Michael Keane and Davy Klaassen but all eyes were on Rooney. The jury was out on his return. Many saw it as him just picking up a hefty pay cheque to top up his pension and a way of slowly winding down his glittering career. 'Never go back' was one of the golden rules of football, with José Mourinho's return to Chelsea being the best recent example of the folly of doing so. Wayne had been pulverising Premier League defences for fifteen years but did he still have the desire to go on as he neared his thirty-second birthday?

The spectre of Jimmy Peter Greaves, the legendary Tottenham and England goal machine, hung over Rooney's career. The stats indicated that Rooney was England's greatest striker but on a percentage basis Greaves was the best finisher. The ex-Tottenham striker was destined to become one of the most exceptional goal-scorers in the history of the game. At his peak Greaves was all quicksilver and energy, cutting through shattered defences like a laser beam. At thirty-one, disillusioned by the increasing demands of the game and in the throes of the alcoholism that almost destroyed him, Jimmy had quit top-level football. Thirty-one could be said to be a dangerous age for a striker. Many saw Rooney as a busted flush, burnt out by years of living in the headlines and blitzed by the pace of the modern game.

The former England captain could have taken the easy

way out by opting for the 'slow boat to China' and untold riches along the way. The MLS (the American organisation Major League Soccer) had also beckoned, promising a life of sunshine, rich living amongst those with perfect white teeth and flawless fashion sense, and well away from the constant scrutiny he received from the British media. Instead he had opted to return to his spiritual home on Merseyside. He had a lot to prove, indeed the expectations could not have been greater, and the consensus was that it was going to be very difficult for him to 'go back to the future'.

In the later stages of the second half of the game, Stoke pushed up, trying to salvage a point. Wayne was visibly tired in the heat but he dropped deeper to put in some strong tackles and preserve their lead. A fine save by the new goalkeeper Pickford from the shot by the Stoke danger man Xherdan Shaqiri also helped to clinch the points.

At the end of the game Rooney spoke to the *Daily Star*:

> There is a lot of expectation coming back here. There are still some fans who maybe thought that I was not good enough to come back here but it is up to me to prove myself.
>
> I have been working hard and I am ready for that challenge to prove myself. I could have gone to another Premier League team and taken my foot off the gas and seen the last few years out. But coming back here I have got to be the best I can be.

The player who slept in 'Toffees' pyjamas had one dream left: he wanted to bring glory back to Goodison Park. Everton fans loved players who gave total effort. No one could doubt Rooney's contribution to games. He offered a different version of the modern player to the new generation of fans. These people had grown up after the decline of heavy industry in the city of Liverpool. Wayne was a reference point to the change in the game. The mistake most made though was to sanctify him. However, the truth was that Everton needed forward players who could supplement his lack of pace.

On Monday 21 August Everton went to the Etihad Stadium to play Manchester City. It was a happy hunting ground for 'The Toffees', who had been beaten in just three of their last ten League visits. It was a fascinating contest that included the meeting of the two ex-Barca legends: Pep Guardiola and Ronald Koeman. Between them they had totalled 455 League games for the Catalan giants, Pep with 263 and Rooney's new boss had clocked up 192. Koeman told the *Daily Telegraph* about his former teammate, saying: 'The way he likes to play is the most difficult way. It's really a pleasure to see his teams playing football.'

Guardiola had spearheaded a wonderful period for FC Barcelona, the most triumphant time in their entire history. In his four-year reign he had won a staggering fourteen trophies out of the nineteen on offer. His spell in Germany managing the most financially sound club in the world, Bayern Munich, was less successful. Whilst sustaining Die Roten (The Reds as this team were known) for domestic supremacy, he had failed to navigate them to their coveted sixth Champions League victory.

Now he was at oil-rich 'City' but his first season in English football had been an expensive let-down, as they failed to win anything. The pressure on him to succeed this time around was immense.

Koeman was in the same boat, call it the *Titanic*, if you like. Just like that ill-fated liner, Koeman should never have left Southampton.

In the opening minutes Rooney almost conceded an own goal as City's free kick, a dangerous effort taken by Kevin De Bruyne, bounced off him. Pickford did well to gather the ball to avoid a sticky moment as Agüero hovered.

On a dark and stormy night the game started under a cloud of smog caused by the pre-match fireworks. The home crowd were soon onto Wayne's case, booing him whenever he touched the ball. Early in the game Schneiderlin brought down the chief City threat Agüero as he threatened to break away. It was an obvious yellow card but Wayne protested to the referee, which incensed the locals. Actually it was not that much of an issue, but when he won a corner midway through the first half and took it, the boos rang out volubly.

The diehard City aficionados had not forgotten his exploits against them when he played for their quieter neighbours. The wonderful bicycle kick that won the Manchester Derby in February 2011 springs to mind. It had recently been voted in the top three of the most visually satisfying great Premier League goals of the past decade.

It was the one where Wayne's body angled like a pair

of scissor blades to blur it past Joe Hart. Over the years Joe had been looking increasingly puzzled at the amount of shots that had beaten him, but this one he found totally bewildering. We know what follows: the sprint to the corner flag and the arms stretching. Then Wayne disappeared beneath, congratulating red-shirted teammates.

Of course, there's nothing new in football. Jimmy Greaves's first goal for Tottenham Hotspur was on his debut for them against Blackpool half a century before, and it had been a scissor-kick, and had been delivered with similar power and precision. Spinning beneath a long throw from the legendary Dave MacKay, Greaves propelled himself upwards, his legs criss-crossing to volley high into the net. Liberated from the nightmare of his time in Milan he kept up his incredible record of scoring a goal on every debut he ever made at every level. Greaves had picked up the scissor-kick trick in the training camp of AC Milan, whilst watching the South American imports. These players spent the hot languid afternoons specialising in unique gimmicks and gymnastic finishing when meeting angled crosses.

Greaves could be credited with being the first British player to bring the bicycle kick into the domestic game. By the time Rooney was in his golden years at Old Trafford he had cultivated the theatrical style which helped to make him the most feared attacker in the Premier League.

That night Man City were seen as clear favourites to win the game, being well odds-on. One of the members of their expensive strike force of Sergio Agüero, Gabriel Jesus and Leroy Sané was expected to open the scoring. Wayne

Rooney was 11–1 to score first in the game, and if you had predicted the correct score on the night, you would have got back almost a hundred times your stake.

But score he did and what a landmark strike it was. David Silva was millimetres away from scoring as he rattled the Toffees' near-side post. The ball was cleared up-field, where the left-wing back Leroy Sané (with the Afro hairstyle) lost the ball. The wide player had been switched to wing-back in the absence of the injured Mendy, who had recently been signed from Monaco. It seemed a strange move but Guardiola liked to be different. This was the man who had used the famous right-back Philipp Lahm as a defensive midfielder at Bayern.

The loss of the ball allowed Dominic Calvert-Lewin to turn Kompany inside-out and square it to Rooney. Our hero instantly dispatched it into the net, the shot spinning off City's new keeper Ederson, then off the post and into the back of the net. It was his 200th Premier League goal, and Wayne became only the second player to reach that figure in its twenty-five-year history.

The goal was observed by England coach Gareth Southgate, who had been sitting in the main stand, checking out players for his World Cup qualifiers and a potential trip to the following summer's World Cup in Russia. The goal triggered an outcry from sections of the media that Rooney should be included in the squad and kindled the idea that he might provide additional firepower for the England attack. Speculation was rife that one of the reasons for Wayne returning to Everton was that he would be playing on a regular basis. Southgate had already announced that no player would be considered for selection if he was not a regular starter for his club side.

Another legendary England striker, Gary Lineker, tweeted after Wayne's goal that, 'There was life in the old dog yet.'

Two of Rooney's former Manchester United managers were also in the crowd to watch him: Sir Alex Ferguson and José Mourinho. Both had been of the opinion that they had seen the best of him at Old Trafford. It was common knowledge that in Ferguson's last season in charge he was keen to sell him. The self-styled 'Special One' used Rooney as a pawn in his game to lure Everton's star striker to Manchester.

Before the game there was a minute's silence to remember the victims of the Manchester Arena suicide bomb attack and the terrorist atrocity in Barcelona. Like the rest of the players on the field Rooney wore a black armband and had a Bee embroidered on his shirt.

Man City had dominated the game in the early stages but Rooney's strike had stunned them. Worse was to follow when their brand new England wing-back, Kyle Walker, was dismissed from the game just on half-time. Walker had been signed for £50 million from Tottenham to give more pace and power on the flanks. After picking up two yellow cards in as many minutes the referee had no option but to send him off. Guardiola was incensed by the referee's decision and remonstrated with the officials, before he quickly reorganised his side, sacrificing his latest hot-shot striker, Gabriel Jesus, for the ex-Liverpool wide player Raheem Sterling.

Everton dropped deeper in the second half, inviting City onto them and hoping to hit quickly on the break. On the hour Gylfi Sigurdsson (making his debut for Everton) came on for Tom Davies but found it hard to make any real impact in the game. Signed from Swansea for £45 million, he was booked for dissent. Questions had been raised at the time of his transfer over the size of his fee and the fact that he played in a position already occupied by Rooney and Davy Klaassen.

Rooney was Everton's best player. The stats indicated that he was covering more ground than any of his teammates and was a constant threat to the City defence. In the later stages of the game the ten men of City launched a relentless late offensive to try to save a point. Eight minutes from time the substitute Sterling volleyed home the equaliser. It looked like Everton would take all three points until another of City's new boys, Danilo, crossed for Holgate to head clear but excruciatingly the ball went only as far as the England winger.

Shortly afterwards Everton's Morgan Schneiderlin was dismissed for a second yellow-card offence after bringing down Sergio Agüero. This left both teams with ten men at the end of the game.

Muhamed Bešić replaced Rooney a minute before the end. The latter had visibly tired and was jeered off the pitch by the City fans. The former England striker took an age to leave the field, milking every last second from the moment,and basking in Everton fans' applause, like a pop star on his final encore. Guardiola embraced him on the touchline, and he looked disarmed. Wayne embodied all the attributes the Catalan prized above all others: football intelligence, total dedication, mental toughness, sheer persistence and an element of rebelliousness.

Guardiola had always been impressed by Rooney's talent and it would have been fascinating to see him play in one of his teams. Perhaps he would have played him in the 'false 9' position, that Leo Messi made his own for Barca. Rooney was always at his best not only prowling in the penalty box, but playing deeper and arriving there at the culmination of an intricate attack.

Pep's nemesis Mourinho had already left the building when Sterling scored. The match had been featured on Radio 5 live and former Snooker World champion and Everton fan John Parrot, who had attended the match, was interviewed and commented that, 'It was great to have him back.'

City were many people's idea of Premier League champions and were widely expected to regain it. A fighting draw on their home ground was a great result for the Toffees. After dropping points, Guardiola's team went on a winning streak that lasted months. Things looked very bright for Everton and the rejuvenated Rooney. Indeed they were so bright he could almost have worn a pair of his wife's 'Prada' sunglasses.

Sky Sports interviewed Rooney at the end and asked him how he felt. In his words:

Frustrated. Going 1–0 up and with the extra man we felt that we could see it out. City created a lot of good chances, our plan was to try and frustrate them, but they have good players that can switch positions. [It's a] difficult job away at City. [The] manager has made it clear that he wants me to play in any of the attacking positions. I want to play games, get match fitness. I think I paid the price last season of not having match fitness.

The interview was concluded by the reporter asking him what it was like to score again at the Etihad.

What? Again?

CHAPTER 2

WHEN WE WERE YOUNG

'The absurd does not liberate; it binds.'
ALBERT CAMUS

The career and life of Wayne Rooney are inseparable from his Irish heritage. Most of the aspects of his character were shaped by that. It fuelled his notorious temperament; more importantly, it influenced his football.

Rooney was always vague about his roots. Even in his autobiography he states that in his early life he was unaware that he was possibly of Irish descent. His father, also named Wayne, was one of eight children and was born in Croxteth, Liverpool, in 1963. This was about the time that The Beatles were beginning their domination of the world. Wayne senior's father was born in Bootle but there the trail apparently ended. Wayne's great-grandfather was most likely to have been one of the huge influx of Irish immigrants that arrived in the mid-nineteenth century.

These folk headed for the major English cities: London, Manchester and Liverpool. Many used the port as the first stage of their emigration to the United States of America. People from that generation never wanted to be farmers again, as they had lost faith in the land that had failed their ancestors and given rise to the Great Potato Famine of the 1840s. Millions of desperate Irish people crossed the Irish Sea to avoid hunger and disease. Many Catholic families settled in Liverpool, particularly in the Scotland Road area. Wayne junior's father was a Roman Catholic, though not strict in his religious views. The immigrants accepted any job they could get, especially occupations in the rapidly expanding seaport.

The influence of the Irish on the culture of Liverpool cannot be underestimated. The distinct accent peculiar to Liverpudlians was a hybrid of the Irish and Lancashire dialects. The most common nickname for Liverpool folk was 'Scouser', and their accent was described as 'Scouse'. Scouse was a type of beef or lamb stew; many thought it was a variant of Irish stew but in fact the term was derived from the word 'Lobscouse', a stew made by nineteenth-century sailors in Northern Europe.

The very name of Rooney was a Gaelic baby name. It meant 'red-haired' and early pictures of Wayne show him sporting a red crew cut. It was a tradition in the Rooney family for the first-born son to be given the name of the father.

The most famous Rooney other than Wayne was the American actor, comedian and vaudevillian, Mickey. He was born Joseph Yule Jr but adopted the name Rooney when he made his film debut at the age of six. His roller-coaster career spanned nine decades, making him the most enduring performer in the history of show business. As the first egocentric teenager to be nominated for an Oscar, his life was a metaphor for that of Wayne's. Ups and downs, marked by precipitous declines and storming comebacks.

Some Rooneys emigrated to America in the 1840s to escape the Irish Famine and established their roots in Pittsburgh, Pennsylvania. They went on to own the franchise of the Pittsburgh Steelers in the NFL (National Football League).

The Liverpool-based Rooneys loved football of a different species though. At the time of Wayne's birth in 1985 there was no Catholic or Protestant split between Everton and Liverpool football clubs.

Everton originated from the community around St Domingo's Methodist Church, and when it became Everton Football Club, players from all religions were welcome. The club just represented the district and everyone in it. The Mersey clubs enjoyed support from both denominations; they had a knack of taking the local experience and the local mindset and rendering it both visible and invaluable. Always the best argument against any sectarian divide between the two clubs was the famous intra-family split. Members of the same family would have different allegiances, with half the household members decked in red, and the other half in blue. This would therefore make it impossible for there to be any sectarian differences within families who were of the same religion.

There were no different allegiances or emotional

dramatics in the Rooney household. Blue was the colour for all of them. Wayne's father grew up at the time of the great Everton team of the late sixties that featured the 'holy trinity' midfield of Ball, Kendall and Harvey. The latter two men were to have a huge influence on young Wayne's career. To this day the standards they set and the football they played are the yardstick by which all subsequent players are compared. The Everton fans of that time gorged themselves on the special talents and fundamental genius of arguably the most alluring midfield team ever. The club had earned the label of 'The School of Silence' and by the time Wayne was growing up, they were known as the 'Dogs of War'.

Wayne's mother Jeanette was one of nine children. The family were as staunch Everton fans as the Rooneys were. Wayne was born on 23 October 1985, making him a Libran, which is the seventh astrological sign of the Zodiac. The main characteristic of a Libran is said to be 'balance', and it was the only zodiac constellation in the sky that was represented by an inanimate object, namely the scales of justice.

That year saw the first episode of the soap opera *EastEnders* being broadcast on BBC One television. It is still running to this day and is Wayne's favourite television show. The Tommy Hilfiger brand was also established at that time. Other famous sports stars born that year included the Croatian midfielder Luka Modrić and record-breaking F1 driver Lewis Hamilton. Notable deaths in 1985 had amongst them the first celebrity AIDS victim Rock Hudson, as well as Yul Brynner, the actor who played the principal gunslinger in the memorable Western film *The Magnificent Seven*.

WHEN WE WERE YOUNG

The Live Aid pop concerts staged in London and Philadelphia raised millions for famine relief in Ethiopia. The movie *Back to the Future* had opened in American theatres and ended up as being the highest-grossing film of the year. By coincidence this sci-fi comedy was set in the same month that Wayne was born.

A few days before Wayne's birth, Everton had been beaten 1–2 at Stamford Bridge in front of a crowd of 27,634. Kerry Dixon and David Speedie scored for the West London side with Kevin Sheedy, a throwback to the glory days, replying for the Toffees. The side put out by manager Howard Kendall was as follows: Neville Southall, Gary Stevens, John Bailey, Kevin Ratcliffe, Pat Van Den Hauwe, Kevin Richardson (sub Adrian Heath), Trevor Steven, Gary Lineker, Graham Sharp, Paul Bracewell and Kevin Sheedy.

This chapter was written in the autumn of 2017, at the time Everton were in the bottom three, with eight points: their worst tally after nine games since 2005/06. Compare the team that Everton played against Chelsea in the Carabao Cup (also a 1–2 defeat) against their eighties counterparts. Ignoring the subject of this book, you could make a case for a complete whitewash by Kendall's team. Certainly, in midfield and up front, it was a kaleidoscope of mediocrity.

Everton finished second to Liverpool that season, losing the League by two points. West Ham finished third, with Chelsea trailing in sixth place. A glance at the League table indicates that it included teams like Oxford, Luton and Coventry, who were long consigned to the obliviousness of the lower leagues.

Getting back to Wayne's family, he had two younger brothers: Graeme and John. The middle brother, Graeme, was named after Graeme Sharp, the legendary centre-forward who helped Everton win two league titles in the eighties. Wayne Snr had two favourites: the Scottish International, Sharp, and Adrian Heath. Comparisons to the team's present-day strikers he considered to be sacrilegious. In fact, he was keen to name his first-born son after him, however his wife, Jeanette Rooney, talked her husband out of this, and Wayne was always glad that she did. How his career would have panned out if he had the moniker of 'Adrian' is just a matter of speculation.

Actor Ray Liotta advised us at the start of the Martin Scorsese seminal gangster film *Goodfellas* that: 'As far back as I could remember I always wanted to be a gangster.'

As for Wayne Rooney, as far back as he could remember he always wanted to be a footballer, and he was kicking a ball as soon as he could walk.

Wayne was brought up in a three-bedroom council house which backed onto a youth club called The Gems. Its chief attraction was a five-a-side pitch made out of plastic, which was very much in vogue back then. Soon the little guy was clambering over his back fence to boot a plastic ball about on the pitch. It all began there and led him to the stratosphere of the modern game.

The first ball he had was a beach ball, which was so lightweight that it would fly in any direction when booted. The freckle-faced kid would spend hours just practising his shooting from any angle, with either foot. Soon he was progressing to a leather ball, bought for him by his Uncle Eugene, because the plastic pitches soon wore out the plastic balls, necessitating the upgrade to leather. It was a Mitre ball, the same one his beloved heroes used.

Wayne's first visit to Goodison Park was when his father took him at the age of six months, and Wayne's father always tried to attend as many home matches as he could. He worked as a general labourer in the building trade and struggled to make a decent living, finding work on the various construction sites in and around the city centre. Work was sometimes in short supply; nevertheless after meeting his family's financial obligations, he did his utmost to see his team play.

The core of the life of the Irish immigrants could often be the struggle to overcome the hardships of their daily lives. It was also about how they found their consolations, whether it was in drink, gambling or the fanatical support of their local football team.

Football provided a unique form of unity to the local community, and it also allowed people from every religion or every ethnic group to share common emotional experiences. Wayne senior was anxious that his eldest son should be exposed to these influences and be absorbed into the community. The impact on him at such an early age was immense, and he was transfixed by Everton Football Club. And he still is.

Wayne's father carried him in his arms to the ground, and the journey required them to travel on two crowded buses. Once inside Goodison Park he had to cradle his son throughout the length of the match. In his wildest dreams Mr Rooney could not have imagined that the son he held in his arms would grow up to be one of its greatest ever players and indeed a legend, on a par with the likes of Dixie Dean and Alan Ball.

Towards the end of the Europa League defeat in October 2017 an Everton supporter, who was holding a toddler, appeared to strike a Lyons player. The Everton player, Ashley Williams, had previously caused a scuffle by barging into Anthony Lopes, the Lyons goalkeeper. Consequently, the custodian crashed into the advertising hoardings and a melee ensued. The main protagonists were Mirallas, the fan with the child, and the Lyons coaching staff. Jordan Pickford ran the length of the field to become involved.

Wayne had been rested for that tie and watched proceedings from the warmth of the executive box. The pictures of the skirmish were shown worldwide and drew the usual outraged responses. It seems that thirty-two years on from Wayne's birth, little had changed. The point was though that fans took their offspring to matches from a tender age in order to indoctrinate them in the culture of Everton Football Club.

They say first love never dies. Wayne had two first loves: Coleen, the girl he married, and his ongoing love affair with Everton Football Club. One of his earliest photographs is of him sporting a huge Everton rosette to celebrate their appearance in the historic 1986 Cup Final. This was the famous Merseyside Cup Final, the first time the giants had clashed in such a match. It's strange that you do not see rosettes at football anymore, but back in the day every fan sported one, the larger the better.

As he grew up more and more Everton merchandise filled up his bedroom: wallpaper, posters, even the lampshade. But what took pride of place on his wall was a team photograph of Everton that included his favourite player, Duncan Ferguson.

The stories about Ferguson are the stuff of legend, for he is a football deity. A larger-than-life character, he held the joint record for the most red cards in the Prem. He had a physique that was sheer Michelangelo, with a larger-than-life personality. To put his influence into context, the club had gone into a gradual decline since the end of the eighties. The Toffees were sinking lower and lower in the Premier League: sixth, ninth, twelfth and thirteenth. In season 1993/94 they were poised on the edge of the abyss, and they only just avoided relegation in the last match of the year.

Ferguson arrived the following season and was the answer to the prayers of the Goodison Park faithful. Initially signed from Glasgow Rangers on loan, he soon won them over with his pace, power and attritional playing style. Ferguson had something that Rooney was to achieve later: an enormous affinity with the crowd. When he turned up at Goodison 'Scots Dunc' was already decidedly a character. The big man had a taste for what the denizens of Glasgow called *Electric Soup*, a Scottish underground humorous comic book series, similar to the English publication *Viz*. Rooney was hugely influenced by the Scottish striker and later on in this narrative we shall examine why. In a special

OK! magazine years later, Duncan Ferguson could be seen looming in the background of the photos at Wayne and Coleen's wedding in Portofina.

Wayne senior soon spotted his son's talent. Sometimes after work he would watch the children playing football in The Gems. One player stood out in all the games: he was travelling yards quicker than the others as adrenalin shot through his body, he had a cannonball shot in either foot and could jump higher than anyone else. It was his first-born son. Before long he arranged for Wayne Junior to play for an Under-9's team run by his local public house. The youth team was called Copplehouse and managed by a character called Big Nev. The standard was high and the big two Mersey clubs used it as a kind of nursery for encouraging future talent. It was a happy and supportive place to first start playing.

Wayne had an instant impact, playing in the same role as his idol Ferguson, smashing in goals with his quick feet and leaping high to head home others. Wayne senior would watch all of these goals sail in, since he never missed a game, no matter what the weather was like. 'Objectivity' was Big Nev's watchword and his young striker only had one object in mind: putting the ball into the net as quickly and as often as possible.

After one particularly hard-fought encounter against one of Copplehouse's main rivals Wayne scored the winning goal in the dying seconds of the game. It was like giving the cat another goldfish. His father was clapping him off when he was approached by a senior citizen, who introduced himself as a scout from Liverpool. Wayne Senior had seen this man before at some of the games, and had thought he was a pensioner who was just passing the time. In fact, he was the best scout since the Apache warriors that used to work for the Native American fighter, Geronimo. He was quick to offer Wayne a trial at Melwood, Liverpool's training centre.

Young Wayne had mixed feelings about his first shot at the big time. Naturally he was delighted to be chosen for a trial at that level. This was tempered by the fact that such was his love for Everton that he felt deep down that in some manner he was betraying them. Very subliminal of course, but perhaps this was the reason why he turned up at Melwood in his Everton strip. Apart from his school uniform this was his main form of attire. He literally spent every spare moment either playing football with his mates or practising his football skills. On his first birthday he had been presented with an Everton kit, and since then he had worn a new one each year. Today he probably would have had a Number 9 on his back with Ferguson's name emblazoned above.

The kit did not go down very well with the Liverpool coaching staff. I once went on a tour of Barcelona's Camp Nou, and amongst our party was a chap who chose to wear a Real Madrid shirt for the occasion. I will always recall the stares he received that afternoon. It seems strange that Wayne's father did not choose a different strip for him to attend the Liverpool trial in. Perhaps it was a deliberate act of provocation: to go inside the enemy's citadel in Blue.

Everton supporters were always bitter that some of the

greatest players in the history of Liverpool were Everton fans, the classic example being Michael Owen. You could also add the names of Robbie Fowler, Ian Rush and Steve McManaman. Wayne was never given the chance to make an impact on the other side of Stanley Park though. Liverpool had seen enough of Wayne's talent to ask him back for more training. The chief Everton scout, with sharper ears than Dr Spock, had heard that their biggest rivals were already courting the hottest young property in town. A call was made to his home and he was invited up to their training ground in Bellefield for a trial. It was the start of a beautiful friendship.

CHAPTER 3

THIS IS ENGLAND
2017

'I have seen some debate around "is he a legend or isn't
he?" If you are the most capped outfield player and record
goalscorer I am not sure what else you have to do to be
called a legend. He said he had been thinking long and
hard about the decision. He feels a sense of loyalty to the
club (Everton) for what they have invested in him.'

GARETH SOUTHGATE

LATE SUMMER

After scoring twice in his first two games for Everton at
the start of the season there was a clamour for Wayne to
return to the England fold. In the previous season Southgate
had dropped him from the National squad as he struggled
to retain his place in the Manchester United team as his

career wound down at Old Trafford. When he moved back to Everton it was speculated with some glee that he was fleeing the scrutiny of the press.

Michael Keane, Everton's new signing from Burnley, believed that Wayne was enjoying a new lease of life since his return to the club. Michael spoke to the *Metro* stating that, 'He deserved a recall to the England squad for the forthcoming World Cup qualifiers.' They were due to play Malta and Slovakia.

'He wants to do really well for this club,' Michael went on. 'He wants to help us win something. Until that happens he won't be resting. He has been fantastic since day one. He is a leader in the dressing room, he has worked really hard on his fitness and it is showing in the games. He has shown his quality as well as his leadership skills.'

Southgate obviously had a dilemma. Should he stick with Rooney, a former England captain, and try and build the team around him or opt for younger blood? In a way it mirrored the situation Everton boss Ronald Koeman was facing at that precise time. Both were in a difficult position in that whatever decision they took, they would be criticised and faced with a peculiarly angry commentary. Koeman's louche indifference to criticism only adding petrol to the fire that was soon to engulf Goodison Park.

For Southgate it meant sticking by the old guard who, however it was dressed up, palpably failed to deliver. Rooney was the figurehead of the so-called 'golden generation' of Frank Lampard, Wayne's close friend Steven Gerrard, the Coles – Joe and Ashley, Terry and Rio Ferdinand. Wayne's

International career was a phantasmagoria of inexplicable oddities. He had played in three World Cups and three European Championships. In those tournaments, or should we say calamities, he had scored seven goals but England were never close to winning anything. The lost boys of England, wastrels of rare talent, were judged to have fallen short. There was a certain sadistic delight in the media's cataloguing of their failures.

Wayne's England career had appeared to be over when Southgate had failed to include him in any of the squads in 2017. It was reported though that Southgate wanted to include him in the squad for the Malta and Slovakia games. However, when he rang Wayne to invite him along to the squad, Wayne broke the shock news that he was retiring from International football.

The news reverberated around the football world. It was a shock because most fans expected the indomitable Rooney to be in the squad for the forthcoming World Cup, largely because they knew his passion for his country and his hunger for gaining wins for England. It must have been a very difficult decision for him to have quit his England career at that point. For many observers, Wayne seemed to be frozen in time and was still the same as when he first appeared on the scene: young, belligerent and indestructible. The very idea of Rooney retiring seemed somehow absurd, yet it served as a reminder to us that age is a process of increasing frailty.

Perhaps deep down the player knew that he was no longer able to compete at the highest echelons of International football and was aware of his encroaching decrepitude. He wanted to quit at the top rather than endure a slow decline. Wayne was at the stage of his career where he was discarding roles that no longer satisfied him. The cornerstone of his life was now Everton Football Club. The World Cup was fool's gold for England, always unattainable but glistening tantalisingly.

After all, as a Tom Stoppard character once reminded us, every exit is an entrance to somewhere else. Wayne was going to make a new start at Everton free of the burden of carrying the weight of the public's International expectations and demands on his broad shoulders.

In an interview published in the England v Slovenia European Qualifier in November 2014, Rooney opened his heart. The England captain candidly admitted that the only thing that would make him believe his England career was a success was, 'Winning a trophy. I could say I have got 200 caps and one hundred goals for my country but the ultimate is to win a trophy. That is why we play football, to win. That is the target, and hopefully sometime soon we can achieve that.'

With his young career at Everton progressing rapidly Rooney had been included in an England Under-15s zsquad for their Victory Shield campaign in 2000. The first game he played in was against Wales, where he came on as a substitute. Wayne was disappointed because he wanted to start in his usual position up front. The deluded England coach at the time did not see his role there and wanted to use him as a winger. For the next match though, he played him as a centre-forward and he scored against Scotland.

The match was televised and his family and friends were watching the star in the making score for the first time in a Three Lions shirt. It all started for him England-wise there. He tasted what it was like to be on TV and to have everyone watch him strut his stuff. Perhaps, far too soon, he had been co-opted into celebrity culture.

In September 2015 England were leading 1–0 against Switzerland in a Euro qualifying tie. The goal had been scored by the sturdy young Tottenham striker Harry Kane, tipped by the media to be a coming force in the game. Clear-eyed Harry was already planning to be a marquee name, therefore decided to build a 'trophy room' at his new house. This was because he needed extra space to house his growing collection of honours and memorabilia.

Wayne already had a trophy room in his mansion and Harry was going to text him to enquire the details of how he had built it. The Nabokovian twist in this was that Kane was seeking advice from Rooney, a man who had been put on a pedestal by the media from an early age because of his daring and power. The trouble was that despite such a meteoric rise, his England career seemed marked by a sense of unfulfilled promise. By contrast, Kane reminds me of a particularly well regarded head prefect at a school, acting as the perfect foil for the grimly ideological headmaster, Southgate.

Kane was twenty-four years old when Wayne returned to Everton. In the 238 games Harry had played in top-class football he had scored 124 goals. That earned him a percentage of 0.52. At the same age Wayne had played in more games – 315, in fact – but had scored fewer goals: 114, thus giving Wayne a percentage of 0.36. Greaves leads the class of twenty-four (who else?) with a massive haul of 251 goals scored in 308 games (a percentage of 0.81). His nearest rival was the Barcelona megastar Lionel Messi, who at that age had scored 180 goals in 269 games (with a percentage of 0.67).

Later on, during a dull game, England were awarded a penalty and up strode England's most famous footballer to convert the kick. Wayne Rooney had now reached the half-century of goals scored for his country – a record-breaking moment that the majority of the crowd had come along to witness and to have a memory to share with their grand-kids. The striker was now the all-time top scorer for England, having passed Sir Bobby Charlton's long-standing record of forty-nine goals. Rooney had admitted that he was never going to be as big a legend as Sir Bobby – because he had won the World Cup with England. To eclipse him, Rooney would have also had to win the World Cup.

Smashing the record had the effect of relegating TV pundit Gary Lineker into third spot, with forty-eight goals. Lineker sent Rooney a tweet of congratulation.

This was a dozen years on from his first England goal in a Euro qualifying tie against Macedonia that made him the youngest Three Lions goal-scorer, at seventeen years and 317 days. England were trailing to Gjorgji Hristov's first-half goal, but eight minutes after the break it was time for Wayne to open his account in the 'Bank of England'. A long ball forward was nodded on by Emile Heskey, who headed down into the path of the active youngster arriving on the edge of the penalty box. He hit the ball sweetly but to this day he feels that the keeper should have saved it, as the leather squirmed over the line.

It is on such moments that careers are built. Rooney described it as a massive moment for him. Pictures of the strike show his attacking partner, Michael Owen, alongside him. Everton fan and deadly striker Owen was England's youngest player of the twentieth century when he made his senior International debut against Chile in February 1998 at the age of eighteen years and fifty-nine days.

Marcus Rashford, a teammate of Rooney in his last season at Old Trafford, has the record for being the youngest player to score on his England debut. It took him just two minutes and fifteen seconds to score against Australia in a warm-up match before the Euros 2016. Marcus was just eighteen years and 208 days old.

The match was played at the Stadium of Light, where thirteen years before Wayne had made his spellbinding England debut. He came on in the second half of the Australia game and rammed home what proved to be the winner from a clever pass by Raheem Sterling. Already parallels were being drawn between the two hit men.

Rashford beat the record set up by another Everton legend that had stood for seventy-seven years. Tommy Lawton scoring against Wales when he was nineteen years and sixteen days old. A tremendously accomplished centre-forward, Lawton was another teenage sensation joining Everton from Burnley in 1937, for the then remarkable fee of £6,500. His International career was interrupted by the war, but he scored twenty-two goals in twenty-three games. Lawton was the greatest header of the ball in football history. Everton fans of those sepia times claimed he could literally 'hang in the air' before powerfully heading the shot home.

We live in an age of records and stats that are all just 'a Google' away. It had taken Wayne 107 games spread over a dozen years to achieve this level of greatness. Sir Bobby Charlton had also taken a dozen years to amass his total of forty-nine goals in one game less. Tucked away and almost unnoticed was one of the most telling stats of them all: those for Jimmy Greaves, who scored forty-four goals in just fifty-nine games. It had taken him just eight years.

Broken down into another format, Wayne scored an England goal every 161 minutes. Bobby took a bit longer, 193 minutes. Whereas Greaves scored a goal for England every 117 minutes. The prolific Tottenham forward scored six hat-tricks for England and not a single penalty kick. Wayne never scored a hat-trick whilst wearing the Three Lions on his shirt.

Southgate claimed that England players had taken an easy option and hidden behind Wayne Rooney in the past, ruefully stating that:

Wayne has been somebody it may have been easy to

hide behind – because he's the one who has carried the burden. That has been unfair on him.

Now everybody has the chance to take the mantle.

If we are going to be an outstanding team, moving forward, then you need players who are going to step up in the big moments. Step up in games.

Roy Hodgson, the ill-fated ex-England boss, rated Wayne as one of the greatest players he had ever managed. Totally surprised that his former captain had quit the International football scene, he told *The Sun*:

Wayne's a top-class player, there's no question about that. His goal record, his appearance record and his achievements speak for themselves.

I was a little surprised when he retired, I must admit. I thought he'd try and continue to get to the next World Cup but these are the decisions players have to make. But what I do know is England owes him, he owes England nothing.

I know how passionate he is about playing for England – I am very sure he's had good reasons for coming to that decision.

Rooney and Roy Hodgson worked very well together. The forty-two caps Wayne won under Hodgson were more than he managed under the jurisdiction of any other England boss, and he also scored goals in abundance. The table of goal ratios to games reads as follows:

WAYNE ROONEY

	Goals	Caps
R Hodgson	25	42
F Capello	14	33
S McClaren	3	7
G Southgate	0	3
S Allardyce	0	1

The tributes to him were 99 per cent positive but in general for England he was underappreciated. The praise of his wonderful achievement was tempered by critics who absolutely believed that when he first burst on the scene with Everton he may have been comparable to the likes of Greaves and Messi. Comparisons were even drawn with Pelé, who is surely the greatest player of all time – a Brazilian International at sixteen and the star of the 1958 World Cup at seventeen. Who could live up to that? At that point in his remarkable trajectory Rooney was identified with the public who watched Everton's games. He never lost his popular roots with the fans who adulated him.

Wayne was the yardstick by which the young strikers were going to be compared to, an epoch. Over the coming months Southgate gave chances to promising young rookies such as Tammy Abraham and Dominic Solanke to showcase their talents. Whether they could reproduce them on the International level at such a young age and follow in Rooney's footsteps was the big question. That was the legacy Wayne Rooney left behind.

He was going to be a hard act to follow.

CHAPTER 4

SMELLS LIKE TEEN SPIRIT

'Which of us has desire? Or, having it, is satisfied?'
VANITY FAIR – THACKERAY

APRIL 1995

The first things he noticed at Bellefield Academy were the photographs on the walls. Pictures of the great moments in the sepia-tinged history of Everton Football Club. He recognised some from the scrapbooks that his father had religiously kept over the years. Mike Trebilcock scoring in the 1966 Cup final win, Andy Gray celebrating winning the European Cup Winners' Cup.

Wayne's father travelled with him on the bus to the training ground. He was no doubt hoping that maybe he could have met Joe Royle, the Everton manager at that time, who was an all-time hero of Wayne senior, and a centre-forward of extraordinary grace and power. Wayne's father had been on the terraces the day a sixteen-year-old Joe had been booed by his own fans for replacing the 'Golden Vision' Alex Young.

By a quirk of fate Liverpool had invited young Wayne along for a second trial on the same evening that Everton had asked to see him. Even though he was in effect 'double -booked', for Wayne there could have only been one choice, Blue being the colour of his preferred team. There was not a club in the world that could have enticed him away from the chance of playing for his beloved Everton.

The trial was similar to the one at Melwood, involving about two dozen kids, most of them dressed in identical Everton kit. Wayne got the gig immediately. From the moment he arrived it was 'Wayne's world', and although it was raining hard, he felt terrific. The trial started with his technique being tested. Wayne demonstrated that he had instant ball control: when the ball came to him he killed it dead, as if it was made of cotton wool. He briefly juggled with it and volleyed it away. Then he called for it again and again. He skipped past defenders in a five-a-side game to smash in a shot that would have taken off the goalkeeper's fingers had he even got near it. Strong, energetic and fast, he put in some powerful runs and sprayed some neat passes. The coaches at Bellefield had seen thousands of wannabes on the never-ending production line of talent, but Wayne literally blew their minds that evening.

Ray Hall was the club's development officer, and his jaws were agape with astonishment when he saw Wayne run the show. At that time there were no hyper-ambitious global scouting systems or aggressive recruitment programmes. In recent years the superpowers of the Premier League, Manchester City and Chelsea, have invested richly in attempting to spawn a generation of youngsters that could compare to those of the majestic Ajax, Barcelona and the Manchester United class of '92. Wayne was born and bred just a bus ride away though, and was to emerge as their finest home-grown product.

The level of Wayne's understanding of the game and technical ability stunned Hall. Even then he was the complete package – a predator and playmaker all rolled into one. Already there was a buzz about Wayne on Merseyside: he was the most talked-about youngster and was seen as a real bright shoot coming through the undergrowth.

Usually Hall had to convince sceptical parents and agents to ignore the common complaints that 'home-grown talents' did not make it on Merseyside. But in Wayne's case there was no hard sell to be made with his parents, and the paperwork was soon completed.

At nine years old Wayne attended training three nights a week after school, on Monday, Wednesday and Friday. The sessions lasted from 5 p.m. to 6.30 p.m. Sunday, however ,was the high spot of the week, because that was when Wayne played in a proper match against other 'academy' sides such as Leeds, Blackpool and of course Liverpool. For the away games the Everton Centre of Excellence Under-10 team assembled at Bellefield and travelled by coach to their destination. Wayne loved travelling to the matches with his pals, for it gave him his first taste of the life of a professional footballer. Boys of that age needed to stand their ground physically or they would have been sunk.

In his first season playing for the Centre of Excellence team he played in thirty matches (two of them were for the Under-11s) and he scored in all but one of them. Wayne was already all pace and raw excitement, running through defences at will. No one could catch him, the defenders being a country mile off the pace. In those days he was like a starving man at an all-you-can-eat buffet, absolutely gorging himself on goals.

Wayne senior was already cataloguing his son's goals and detailing the matches he played in. The Rooney ledger indicated that the only game he did not score in was a 0–0 draw with Bury. This must have been an amazing game bearing in mind the mind-melting scores in some of the other matches, such as Everton 15 – Preston 0 (Rooney 9), Everton 13 – Anglesy 0 (Rooney 8) and Everton 7 – Chester 0 (Rooney 6).

Bury must have had a good goalkeeper that day.

Wayne's best memory of that goal-drenched season was a 12–2 win over Manchester United in which he scored a double hat-trick. The best of the half-dozen was a bicycle kick he scissor-kicked home from a misplaced clearance. With his back to goal there was little alternative for him but the quickness of thought and action that was already characterising his play, and which pocketed him another goal. Already he had started to exhibit his repertoire of convincing and dazzling skills.

The coaches from both sides broke into applause, and

his brothers, John and Graeme, were there too to celebrate the moment. United was the big match of the season for Everton at any level. The Mancs were world-famous for their youth system that had produced a wealth of talent from the doomed Busby Babes to the recent golden generation of Beckham/Giggs/Scholes. Flesh and blood superheroes, they existed in those days too.

The thing that struck Wayne most as he watched the youngsters in tomato red practise their intricate skills before kick-off was that most of them were wearing gloves. Woollen gloves would have been frowned upon in the back streets of Croxteth, even on the bitterest of cold days.

Wayne thrived on the impossible, like all great strikers, such as Pelé, Dixie Dean, and Denis Law, who the United background staff still strived to replace. Perhaps that was the first time that the name of Wayne Rooney was pencilled into their notebooks as a possible heir to the throne of one of their most flamboyant showmen. After all, football is the original 'Game of Thrones'.

Wayne finished with 114 goals for the season, but he was still worried that Everton would retain him for the following year. Confidence was never a problem for him, but such was the high standard of the Everton Academy that there were youngsters there that even Wayne was in awe of. One of them was a midfield player called Joseph Jones. Wayne would talk of him in reverential terms, praising his abundance of skill and great vision. Jimmy Greaves nearly did not sign for Chelsea as a youth team player because of another lad called David Cliss who was on their books at the time. Greaves could not see himself making any progress with Cliss blocking his path, a player whom he regarded as being infinitely better than himself. However, Cliss made a few appearances in the first team before drifting out of football and emigrating. Greaves, just like Rooney, then went on to become a legend in the game, and I have no idea what became of Joseph Jones. Such is the wafer-thin difference between making it at the highest level and being consigned to anonymity.

Being naturally right-footed Wayne knew he had to work on his left side. He was discovering that speed was much more than just the ability to sprint. His talent at running fast was a huge weapon in his armoury but was not sufficient in itself for playing at the highest level. For example, many youngsters could cover ground rapidly but had difficulty in starting, stopping and, most importantly, in changing direction. Goal-scoring chances were lost because of a player's inability to turn quickly.

The coaches worked on strengthening Wayne's legs to make him quicker on the turn but the key was constant practice. A fellow called Dennis Evans looked after Wayne at this level. He had an excellent reputation and was highly regarded by the Everton hierarchy. Wayne never stopped playing football, and he was described as 'the last of the street footballers'. When he had finished training he would go home, have his tea, then go out in the street and play with his pals. He just wanted to play football, and being in the midst of a game was where he was most comfortable.

After what seemed an eternity he received a letter from

Everton, not only telling him that he had been retained in the Academy but that he had been promoted to the Under-12s. Enter Colin Harvey, the youth team manager and Everton legend. When he first went to Bellefield it had been the Co-op's old sports ground and was in a state of dilapidation. The players had to report to Goodison Park and then travel backwards and forwards by mini-bus. After training they had to return to Goodison Park for a shower. All that was to change when the training centre was completely refurbished in 1966 for the World Cup. Everton's home ground hosted games up to the semi-final, and the legendary Brazil team ,including Pelé and Garrincha, trained at Bellefield. The fact that Rooney learnt his craft at that place was ironic. Maybe one day they will put a blue plaque up to commemorate his time there.

Colin Harvey made his first team debut in the 1963/64 season in the European Cup against Helenio Herrera's Inter Milan in the San Siro Stadium. They were a Euro superpower then and went on to win the competition after knocking Everton out 1–0 over two legs. They retained the European Cup the following season.

Harvey was lucky enough to play in front of World-Cup winning full-back Ray Wilson, the prototype wing-back. Alongside him was Howard Kendall and the man he described as the best player in the history of the club – Alan Ball.

Alan called the midfield, the 'Panzer' division, comparing them to the crack German armoured division of World War Two. Akin to little tanks swarming all over their opponents, they were three little guys, totally mobile and intensely committed to the cause of Everton Football Club. All three had agile, quick feet. They were a blueprint for the top twenty-first century Premier sides, making quick exploratory attacks and tracking back fast to carry out defensive duties.

Colin's connection with the club lasted years, and he even managed them for a spell. He was a brilliant, under-rated player brimming with class, brio and brains. Colin was just unlucky in that he did not get the full recognition he deserved, as he played at a time when there were so many talented English midfielders. He won just one full England cap. Looking at the paucity of top-class English talent in that area today (Doug Livermore and Dier played against Brazil in November 2017), Colin Harvey would have walked into the squad.

As Everton's youth manager Colin had master-minded Everton's FA Youth Cup win in season 1997/98. The team included Leon Osman, Richard Dunne, Tony Hibbert, Danny Cadamarteri and Francis Jeffers. That nucleus of the side played over 800 games for Everton and three of them played at International level. Francis Jeffers went to the same school as Wayne and their paths were to entwine over the coming years. Wayne's mother was actually sitting with Franny's mother in church when he first told her the news that he was joining Everton.

Howard Kendall watched the FA Youth Cup-final triumph with a smile on his face. It was his final days as manager but he was happy that the future of the club looked bright, with such a promising crop of youngsters coming through. The sometimes prickly relationship he had forged with Colin had stretched back over thirty years on and off and was now coming to a close. Howard asked him if there was anybody else coming up through the ranks to reinvigorate his squad. He valued Colin's judgement on youngsters, for he had such exacting standards and very, very few players lived up to it.

'Only one,' Colin told him. 'Wayne Rooney, he's just a kid.'

The first time Colin had seen Wayne was one Sunday morning when he went to watch the different age group teams. The priority group were the under-16s and 15s because from those teams the next intakes were made. An injury occurred in the under-16s' game and with play interrupted, Colin strolled across to the under-10s to see what was occurring. He nodded over to Dennis Evans, who was watching the match intently. One of the young Everton players suddenly seized the ball on the halfway line and surged forward.

Colin could not recall who the young Everton side were playing that day, just that they were some team in white. However, what he did remember was the kid dribbling through their defence as if it was a playground kickabout. He finished the run by taking on the biggest of the bunch and, in one move, passing the ball between his legs. Then he unleashed a thunderbolt shot into the roof of the net.

'Who's that?' Colin enquired.

'Wayne, Wayne Rooney,' Dennis replied, wiping his lips on his sleeve, with a kind of reverence in his voice.

Colin was transfixed. Rooney was running in unpredictable directions that completely flummoxed the opposing defenders. Within a quarter of an hour he had scored again after another mazy run, dancing past the flailing legs and firing home a blistering shot. Harvey turned to Dennis with a puzzled look on his face.

'He does that every game, several times,' Dennis told him sardonically.

Harvey walked away. He had seen enough.

Wayne just continued doing what he did best: scoring goals. In John Sturges's seminal Western film *The Magnificent Seven*, the character played by Steve McQueen advised the leader of the banditos (Eli Wallach) that, 'We deal in lead.'

Wayne Rooney dealt in goals.

He joined the Roman Catholic comprehensive school De La Salle as his secondary school, and all the boys there were football mad. As he progressed through the years at the Centre of Excellence he would go to Bellefield Academy some mornings for extra training. Colin Harvey, taking an increasing interest in his progress, would ferry him around. Wayne would be wearing his school blazer when he grabbed some lunch in the canteen. Normally this would have caused some comments from the older players but such was his growing reputation in the club that not a word was said to him. His talent set him apart, yet socially he was not apart from his teammates.

Harvey remembers how humble and taciturn Wayne was in those days. Very shy, he only spoke when he was spoken to. If Harvey did not speak to him when they drove him back to De La Salle, then the journey was conducted in silence. Wayne was particularly shy around any of his heroes if he met them around the club.

Being in the School of Excellence (soon to change its title to the Everton Academy) entitled Wayne to be a ball boy and a mascot. The future captain of England was a ball boy for two years at Goodison Park and had a great view of the matches, as well as the chance to sharpen his reflexes. The ball boys were under strict instructions, to always throw back the ball, but Wayne was more comfortable kicking it to the players. However, in his first game he received a tongue lashing from the club's greatest ever goalkeeper – Neville Southall.

In a career lasting sixteen years the Welsh keeper was second only to Wayne in terms of honours won. Twice winner of the League Championship, one FA Cup triumph, a European Cup Winners' Cup win and a record amount of Welsh caps made him another candidate for a trophy room.

Everton had been trailing in the match but equalised late in the game. Wayne was positioned to patrol the area near the goal that Southall was guarding. With his gaunt cheeks and dark hair, the goalie looked like a scruffy version of the actor, Daniel Day-Lewis. Tactical genius that he was, Wayne believed that the Toffees would settle for a point. So, when the ball went out of play for an Everton goal kick he was in no hurry to return it. He had reckoned without Southall though, who was keen to pick up a win bonus. The Llandudno-born keeper was getting ready to boot the ball upfield in one last charge. The undue delay irked the big Welshman, and he unleashed a torrent of abuse against the hapless ball boy. Wayne was visibly stung by this outburst, especially coming as it was from one of his heroes.

But they used to say that revenge is a dish best served cold, and Wayne got his own back on the 'binman' keeper (his autobiography was entitled the *Binman Chronicles*, referring to his teenage employment as a dustman) later that season. He was offered the role of club mascot for the biggest game of the season: the Merseyside derby against the Red men, the big one, to be played at Anfield. Wayne was beside himself with excitement, his heart thumping like a stolen moped. For him to be appearing on the pitch in the enemy citadel was too much to take in.

Fate intervened though, when torrential rain hit the North East on the day of the big match and the game was postponed. Wayne was heartbroken, and his mother had never seen him so distraught. He had even travelled to the ground through the rain-drowned city when the downpour had ceased and there was a chance of the game going ahead, only for it to be called off as the heavens opened again. On the bus home he stared out at the spokes of trashed umbrellas and bins lying on their sides, wondering if he would ever get a chance to be there again.

Eventually, about a month later, the game was rearranged and Wayne went along to the match. The Everton mascot had to pinch himself to make sure it was actually happening to him, but it was. Wayne was ready hours before his parents took him to Liverpool's ground. Eventually the game started. Just before the players took to the field he was introduced to the Everton captain, Dave Watson. He had seen some of the senior players in the distance when he went to Goodison or occasionally when they were at Bellefield for treatment.

Dave Watson asked Wayne how he was progressing at the Academy, and he mumbled something incoherent in reply, being visibly star-struck and almost overcome with excitement and emotion. The Liverpool captain that day was the icon John Barnes, who gave him a lovely smile. Barnes had risen to prominence at a time when racism was prevalent in the sport. His wonderful skill and courage paved the way for the generation of black players afterwards. One of the most striking images of the late eighties was Barnes back-heeling a banana that was thrown onto the pitch during his team's FA Cup tie with Everton.

Wayne's abiding memory of the mascot day was how small he felt in comparison to the Premier League stars. It was like something out of the old sci-fi show he used to watch with his dad: *Land of the Giants*, and the Liverpool players looked particularly gulp-inducing.

The noise when the teams went onto the pitch was deafening as the punters hollered and stamped their feet. He had never experienced anything like it but it set his adrenalin racing. The Kop roared for their heroes and jeered the Blue Noses. He did not know what he was experiencing but he wanted more.

One of the perks of being a mascot was that you could have a little shoot-out with the Everton keeper before the match. This practice also helped Southall warm up for the game, without exerting him. Wayne had noticed in the home games when he was a ball boy how none of the previous ball boys had ever given Southall anything to worry about. Overcome by it all, the mascots either ended up shooting wide or rolled the ball back tamely for the keeper to scoop up. Wayne had other ideas though, for he had been practising the chip shot for weeks.

Even back then he had the ability to propel the ball over opponents and used it in so many facets of his game. Wayne has always possessed that impudent skill, that paradoxical nature of having a level of extraordinary ability to attempt the spectacular and the football intelligence to recognise the possibility of doing so. Outside the penalty area of one of the most famous pitches in the history of football he sighted the top far corner of Neville Southall's goal and chipped it there with unerring accuracy.

Southall was furious at this humiliation heaped on him by a ten-year-old mascot. He silently swore again at the youngster. Seconds later Wayne chipped him again, stabbing his toe beneath the ball and sending it upwards steeply and imparting a little backspin. This time it clipped the crossbar, with Southall being just another onlooker. The crowd started cheering. Years later, Sky found the footage, recognised the youngster with his socks down and started running it. Southall was still no nearer saving the shots.

CHAPTER 5

BABY, YOU CAN DRIVE MY CAR

'Everybody wants to turn you into a f***ing
d***head, pipe and slippers. I don't f***ing think so.
I've built this f***ing thing. I know when I'm being
out of order and when I'm just doing it for a laugh. I'm
never f***ing changing. Never.'

LIAM GALLAGHER

SEPTEMBER 2017

So Wayne was back at his spiritual home and had scored in his first two games. The distractions of an England career behind him, all he had to do was concentrate on furthering the cause of Everton Football Club and stay out of trouble. What could go wrong?

In the early morning of the first of September Wayne was arrested for drink driving near his £6-million Cheshire home in the village of Prestbury. The story made the front page of every paper in the country. Despite leaving Manchester United and the England set-up he was still the biggest name and the most recognisable footballer in it.

The evening was a jolly boys' outing to give his former Manchester United teammate, Wes Brown, a send-off before he left to play in India. Wes was a good buddy of Wayne's. Born in Manchester, he joined United as a trainee, and had been a key member of their ironclad defence for many seasons. Now in his late thirties, he was heading East to play out his career, and top up his pension plan.

The party also included another ex-Manchester United teammate, Phil Bardsley, and the new Everton keeper Jordan Pickford. 'Bardo' was born in the same year as Wayne but never really made it at Old Trafford, and moved to Burnley. Their friendship was maintained throughout and the pair made the headlines in 2015 when *The Sun* revealed a video of Bardsley knocking out his best chum. This incident occurred in a kitchen 'boxing bout'. The duo had been swapping punches when a left jab that may or may not have troubled Anthony Joshua floored Wayne. Boys will be boys though.

Pickford, the youngest in the group, had joined Everton in the summer from relegated Sunderland. Widely tipped by the experts to take over from the floundering Joe Hart as the number-one goalkeeper in the England team, Jordan had withdrawn from the national team squad through injury. The Blues custodian should have been playing in Malta the following evening in the World Cup qualifier and was deeply upset that he had missed out on the chance of establishing himself as England's first choice.

Perhaps Wayne had similar thoughts about not being in Malta, even regrets that he was no longer part of the England team. The International break meant that Everton had no fixture and Wayne had time on his hands, because Everton manager Ronald Koeman had given him four days off.

A late afternoon Italian meal started proceedings in one of his favourite haunts: the Piccolino in Alderley Edge. Wayne loved Italian food and the football-loving waiters always made a huge fuss of him. The problem was it was almost impossible for any of the players who lived in that 'Cheshire Mansion belt' area to move around without attracting the attention of the paparazzi. They were big fishes in a very small pond.

The chaps eventually moved on to the nearby bar and restaurant called The Bubble Room. The Bubble Room was an apt name; for over half of his short life Wayne had lived in a bubble, scrutinised with a remorseless intensity by the media that might be expected to overwhelm even the most mentally strong. As the evening wore on, Rooney was bellowing out Oasis songs.

The Bubble Room bar had a band playing that night by the name of Funky Treacle. Their lead singer, Neil Shaw, told *The Sun*: 'There was a lot of people drinking and it was a particularly vibrant crowd. When we did "Mr Blue Sky" they were actually booing because they wanted Oasis – so we did "Wonderwall."'

Oasis were Wayne's favourite band, and had been since he was a kid in the backstreets of Liverpool. A few miles down the road in his palatial mansion lay a guitar signed by the song's composer, Noel Gallagher. To illustrate his love for the band, when he was thirteen years old Wayne had to write a letter to a family in Dallas (the eponymous TV series made the town famous). These people were putting him up for a fortnight whilst he played for Everton in a tournament. The youngster had to list his hobbies (although he only really had one hobby: football) and he wrote about listening to his favourite band, Oasis.

Being a fiery character he was attracted to others of a similar nature. Duncan Ferguson, with the outlaw twinkle in his eyes, was his favourite footballer and a kind of hero to the younger man. The Scot had pride of place amongst the pantheon of Wayne's Everton heroes, the players who shaped his 'football DNA'. The Gallagher brothers were musos but were still Wayne's idols and their music became the soundtrack to his childhood. It was part of his foundation, it helped to make him who he was going to be. In later years, if he closed his eyes he was back in the coach going to an away-game playing for the Academy. The radio was on playing Oasis, something about a 'Champagne Supernova'. The energy and simplicity of the song blew his mind, with lyrics such as: 'Where were you when we were getting high?' It was music that made him want to kick Uncle Eugene's leather ball so hard it would disappear from view.

Liam Gallagher had made it from living in a council house in Manchester to getting a record deal and in his glory years performing in front of 250,000 people in Knebworth Park. Rooney always defined success as a triumph over the odds. Now at forty-four, Liam was staging a comeback after going solo. In an interview with the *Evening Standard* at around that time, he spoke of a period after Oasis split up when he 'was drinking too much' and that he: 'Was gonna go and live in Spain and just chill out, eat nice, bit of sun on me bones and just f***ing live.'

The belated emergence of Gallagher as a solo act showed he still had the self-belief and courage to face the spotlight again. Liam had the weight of Oasis still hanging over him. Similarly, Wayne Rooney had the weight of Everton, Manchester United and his country hanging over him.

And so it could be said that Wayne was in a parallel position to that of his favourite singer, in that both men were in danger of collapsing under the weight of their own history, and were hanging onto their careers at the top by their fingernails. In fact Wayne was somehow diminished by leaving the myth of Manchester United and was now cut off from the England team. Perhaps he needed Everton more than they needed him.

Also enjoying Oasis at Bubble Bar was lettings office manager Laura Simpson, from Irlam in Manchester, and at some point in the evening she joined Wayne and his friends. Eventually the group left the bar and went to another one: The Symposium, which was a cocktail bar in Wilmslow, owned by *Hollyoaks* actor Ashley Taylor-Dawson. What exactly transpired next is unclear, but in any event, the evening concluded with Wayne and Laura being stopped by the police in a vehicle near to the cocktail bar in the early hours.

WAYNE ROONEY

The car he was driving was a ten-year-old, black, rag-top VW Beetle that belonged to Laura. It was 2 a.m. and he was pulled over because of a faulty brake light. Wayne was breathalysed and allegedly found to be three times over the legal limit. He was subsequently arrested and spent the night in a police cell.

A Cheshire Police spokesman said, 'The man was arrested shortly after 2 a.m. today after officers stopped a black VW Beetle on Altrincham Road, Wilmslow. Wayne Rooney has since been charged with driving whilst over the prescribed limit. He's been released on bail and will appear at Stockport Magistrates Court on September 16.'

Wayne was released at 1.30 p.m. the following afternoon. Looking forlorn and unshaven, he slumped in the back of the car sent to collect him from Middlewich Police Station. His ear was glued to his mobile.

In the art world the rule of thumb is to separate the art from the artist as a person. In reality though, the public are just as interested in the painter as his paintings. Take Amedeo Modigliani, for example, a man whose exploits made George Best look like a boy scout. He was a hard-living, philandering booze-hound who did not make it to thirty-five. The deadly excess that fuelled his talent consumed it once and for all. Some critics claimed that if it had not been for his philandering lifestyle he never would have received such attention for his artwork. In the world of football the public have a seemingly insatiable appetite to learn details of their heroes' private lives. Over the years Wayne has had to endure details of events he undoubtedly regrets picked over by the tabloids.

Wayne told Coleen that he was just driving Laura home. It would not be surprising if Coleen had questions. Thursday nights were usually the nights that Wayne reserved to take her out, either to the cinema or for a spot of dinner. But Coleen was 1,300 miles away on holiday in sunny Majorca, and that was her seventh holiday of the year. So far that year she had been to Amsterdam, Dubai, Spain, Barbados, Portugal, Mykonos, Ibiza and Italy. Coleen's parents had accompanied her to the Spanish resort.

Coleen Rooney wears dresses from Céline, has an adherence to high heels and adores eye-catching jewellery. She did not always live like that though. Wayne and Coleen first met when a twelve-year-old Wayne played football with her brothers, Anthony and Joe McLoughlin. This was in the next street of stuccoed buildings to his, in the garages behind her home in Croxteth or 'Crocky' as he called it. Their families were friends and Wayne's cousin Claire was a pal of Coleen. The McLoughlins were Irish too, and her granddad hailed from County Mayo.

Wayne first came to Coleen's attention when he broke, accidentally he always claimed, her brother Joe's tennis racket. For this misdemeanour he incurred the wrath of her father, a big Liverpool fan. Mr McLaughlin's proudest moment was travelling to Rome to watch the Red men win the European Cup against Borussia Mönchengladbach, 3–1. (That was the one that Tommy Smith scored in.) For this reason, a budding Evertonian superhero was the last person he wanted his daughter bringing home.

When Wayne told Coleen he was at the Everton

Academy she thought it was some advanced educational establishment, which did not really sit with the impression she had formed of him. Coleen was the swot with eleven GCSEs and a burning ambition to learn Media Studies at Uni. Their first date was when he took her to the Showcase cinema to see Austin Powers. (I am not sure if it was *The Spy Who S****ed Me*.) Knowing his penchant for wearing his Everton kit to most social occasions, Coleen expressly asked him not to do so.

Fast forward to 2017 and Coleen was on holiday with her three sons: Kai aged eight, Klay aged four and Kit, who was almost two. She had recently announced on Instagram that she was expecting a fourth child. After the episode of Wayne's night out that culminated in his drunken driving, Coleen naturally wanted answers.

Wayne had made mistakes in the past, and of a more lurid type. In 2004 he confessed that he visited prostitutes in the early days of their courtship. Six years later, in 2010, with Coleen five months pregnant with Kai, prostitute Helen Wood claimed he had paid her for a threesome with escort Jenny Thompson. Coleen had hoped that the move back to Everton would have been a fresh start for them but this new incident was alarming.

Wayne was facing aggravation from all directions. He drove to Finch Farm for talks with Ronald Koeman, who was another person furious at his star player's behaviour. Before he had re-joined the club, they had a sit-down, during which his lifestyle choices had been discussed at length. Koeman had taken Rooney's word that there would be no problems, and Everton wanted him on the back (sports) page of the newspapers, not at the front. Now, just fifty-three days after sealing the most talked about transfer move of the summer, Rooney had spent the night at the Middlewich Custody Suite after his arrest for drink driving.

Koeman was known for his strict treatment of players and a certain aloofness. A top player himself, he knew that the International break for footballers could turn out to be an International break-out.

Everton's next fixture was a difficult-looking home game against Tottenham Hotspur and he wondered whether or not to include Wayne in the side. Discombobulated by his recent turbulence, Rooney might have been an unwelcome sideshow for Koeman at that stage of the season, and the Dutchman was conscious of the fuss around Rooney the previous November, when he stayed up drinking until 5 a.m. in the England camp. This was following their qualifying win over Scotland.

In the end Wayne was fined two weeks' wages by the club. They avoided prejudicing his court appearance, confining themselves to a prepared statement. Koeman described the club as being 'very disappointed', and a cloud now hung over the resurrection of their prodigal son.

Meanwhile Coleen had been ringing around her friends, trying to establish what exactly had happened that night. She phoned Wes Brown's wife Leanne and Bardo's wife Tanya to try to piece together the story. The wife of Paul Stretford (Wayne's agent) had also been consulted. The Rooneys were always newsworthy, even more so than the Beckhams because of the fact that Wayne was still playing. The Rooneys' relationship seemed, at least from the outside, more colourful than that of the Beckhams too. The torrent of words about Wayne and Coleen was now a super–highway of prose.

Andy Warhol once said, 'In the future, everyone will be world-famous for 15 minutes.' Whether he was correct is debatable, but what is undoubtedly true was that now the media wanted to hear Laura Simpson's account. She went on the Holly Willoughby and Phillip Schofield ITV show *This Morning* to tell her side of things, saying:

> We fell into talking to each other. Basically, we just got a cab. It was a bit of a whirlwind really. There was no conversation.
>
> We just ended up in my car. In my eyes I was a couple of drinks down. It wasn't discussed as to what would happen.

The tabloids were full of conjecture but Laura's own account was clear.

Whatever the reaction of Coleen and Wayne to the interview, the full media glare was focused on the Rooneys now.

Wayne played against Tottenham. The club's failure to replace Romelu Lukaku had left them short of options up front. The week before the International break Everton had played champions Chelsea at Stamford Bridge. They played ineffectively and were easily beaten 0–2. Wayne had found it hard to chase the Chelsea shadows and the manner of the defeat troubled him.

BABY, YOU CAN DRIVE MY CAR

Something told him that it was going to be a hard season. The Goodison faithful were not concerned with his private life or chewing over his off-field behaviour, it was on the pitch where his behaviour mattered to them. They were convinced that Rooney would put in the effort for them as he had always done in the past. The problem was that at his age it needed even bigger sacrifices to meet the required level of fitness.

Everton's shortcomings were ruthlessly exposed by Tottenham, who scored three times in the first half without reply. That was how it finished at 0–3. Everton improved in the second half but were outclassed in all departments.

Wayne had a poor game, earning just four out of ten for his performance. Harry Kane earned double that amount and scored twice to open his account for the season. Mauricio Pochettino, the Tottenham manager, compared Kane to his fellow Argentinian Gabriel Batistuta. Known as 'Batigol', he smashed fifty-four goals in seventy-seven games during his International career and terrorised defences in Italy.

Kane's first goal was a fluke, an intended cross which deceived Jordan Pickford, that took him to one hundred goals for his club. The Everton attack was lightweight and Sandro Ramírez was withdrawn at half-time. Wayne was playing behind him on the right-hand side of midfield but could make no impression. Their midfield was outshone by the Spurs diamond in which Dele Alli was outstanding. As Wayne trudged from the field at the end of two troubled weeks, the thought might have crossed his mind that the road to reparation could be a long one.

CHAPTER 6

RISE OF THE FOOT SOLDIER

'He was flipping Roy of the Rovers at that [youth] level. Some of the stuff he could do; he would just get the ball and run straight through the other team. From the halfway line or something, run straight and score.'

ARCHIE KNOX, FORMER EVERTON ASSISTANT MANAGER

SPRING 2002

Wayne was now fourteen and working his way through the Academy. The previous summer he had captained an Everton youth side that had won a youth tournament in France. The standard was very high as they competed against teams from Brazil and Europe. The first signs of issues that were to cloud his career started to appear at around that time. His strong temperament became more apparent, along with a fierce streak of independence. He was also to suffer his first major injury setback.

WAYNE ROONEY

The Everton Academy held no terrors for him but academically he was struggling. After training on a Monday a special room was allocated to the lads to catch up on their homework. Wayne swerved this by simply saying that he had none. This might have had something to do with the fact that he ended up without a solitary GCSE.

One instance of how his schooldays went was when Wayne bowled into a science lesson, bouncing his favourite football on the floor like a Harlem Globetrotter. Everton did not allow him to play for the school team, so the only time he got to play football in term time was in the lunch break. The teacher confiscated the ball, which was a massive blow to him. Indeed it affected him so profoundly that later that same morning back in the science lab, he kicked a wall panel in, reducing it to a pile of dust. When questioned later about the incident he was caught red-handed when, in best *CSI* fashion, the science teacher observed dust particles on his boots. Wayne was suspended from school for two days for that one.

Not the first young player to consider himself a tactical genius, Wayne also found himself having a rather different view to a new coach who had joined the club. The coach had made a point of instructing him to play in a more defensive manner. Even then, at that level, the pragmatic side of the game was starting to dictate tactics. The youngster was told to train with the defenders, but he protested, insisting that he was a striker and that defending had no part in his game. The coach threatened to drop him from the team's next game, whereupon Wayne's father, always the diplomat, had a long talk with his son and smoothed the matter over.

RISE OF THE FOOT SOLDIER

The Everton management soon realised what a handful Wayne could be when seeking a win – both to defenders, and game officials. He was becoming more frustrated with referees over the lack of protection afforded to him by defenders who could only stop him with cheap fouls. That 'will to win' was coming to the fore and he hated to lose. He took it especially badly if that was caused by a referee's error or a basic mistake by a linesman, and his reputation as a fierce competitor was growing daily.

Then the injury struck. Beginning as a pain in his right knee, it made running virtually impossible and even the slightest movement problematic. He tried to hide it as best he could, but the pain grew worse and in the end he consulted the club physio. The symptoms were instantly diagnosed as Osgood-Schlatter Disease, which in its simplest form is inflammation of the ligaments of the knee – and particularly problematic for athletes involved in running and jumping sports. It had no connection with the legendary Chelsea striker Peter Osgood.

Incidentally, as a youngster Peter had probably been as good a prospect as Wayne, but a badly broken leg at the age of nineteen robbed him of a yard of pace. He never quite fulfilled his awesome potential, although he had a wonderful career at Stamford Bridge and played for England. Peter was another player who had a fiery commitment.

The disease that Wayne had succumbed to was very common in youngsters whose bones are soft and still in the process of growing. The only cure was complete rest and Wayne was out of action for over a month. In that time he did not even kick a ball and his only contact with the game was watching his teammates from the sidelines. It was the longest month of his life and at the end of it he vowed that he would take care of himself better and not lose any more of his precious time.

He soon started where he left off, scoring goals for fun, and he was certainly having plenty of that. Representative honours were starting to come his way. What is more, a run out for Liverpool schools merited headlines and column inches in the local paper. It was spotted by Coleen's dad, who told his daughter that the young boy was looking a likely lad. Soon afterwards he won his first England honour by being called up for the Under-15s. Their opponents were Wales, in a competition called the Victory Shield. The match ended in a dramatic 1–1 draw and Wayne made his debut in an England shirt, coming on for the last half an hour. However, he did enough in that time to be nominated as Man of the Match.

The player he replaced was the winger Wayne Routledge, who was regarded at the time as the cream of the crop. Routledge was a prodigiously talented Crystal Palace player at the time. Fast forward seventeen years to a few weeks before Christmas and Routledge came on as a substitute for Swansea in a grim relegation battle against West Bromwich. Meanwhile, Wayne was starring in the Scouse derby. Routledge had a journeyman career playing for Tottenham Hotspur, Portsmouth, Fulham (both on loan), Aston Villa, Cardiff (loan), QPR (twice, once on loan).

The only other player from the team to make it to the

giddy heights of the Premier was Lee Croft, who played for Manchester City before moving to Norwich, and then Southport. The remaining players failed to reach the next level.

Young Master Rooney played on the right wing during that game, a decision made by Steve Rutter, the coach in charge at that time. Wayne wanted to play in his usual role through the middle, but Rutter did not think he was up to it and switched him to the wing. Wayne always fought his corner when it came to his career, and he was tenacious, plus his drive and ambition were obvious. Nobody knew better than him. How many promising youngsters have had their potential diluted by being played out of position? You shudder to think.

Wayne retained his place in the side though, and scored the first goal in a 5–0 romp over Scotland, and a further goal came against Canada. In all he played six games for the England Under-15s. Great oaks from little acorns grow, as you might say.

In his talkSPORT interview with Alan Brazil in December 2017, Wayne hoped that, 'One or two of the youngsters who had recently made an impact in Gareth Southgate's England team may be going to the World Cup in Russia.' He added a word of caution, saying that although it was an exciting time for England, the youngsters should not be rushed.

The FA Youth Cup was his next priority and in season 2001/02 he led Everton to the final of the competition against Aston Villa. This was the big chance for them to lift the biggest prize in youth football. The team was always looking for him to come up with something special, something that would make a difference.

Peter Osgood had the record for scoring in every round of the FA Cup. Wayne was trying to emulate that by scoring in every round of the Youth Cup. He scored twice against West Bromwich in the fourth round then got another brace against Manchester City.

The City match was watched by Walter Smith, the Everton manager at that time, and his office had a great view of the pitch. Smith had replaced Howard Kendall, after his third stint as Everton manager. It was the last days of his regime and he was about to be replaced by a fellow scot called David Moyes, who had made a big impression at Preston North End. Colin Harvey had given Smith a heads-up about Wayne. At first the ex-Rangers boss had refused to believe that a fifteen-year-old boy was playing in the Everton Under-19 team. This was unheard of even in Scotland, where young talent tended to be pushed through academies at a quicker rate than that of their southern counterparts.

Espying Wayne's performance through his window he drew gasps from the ex-Scotland manager, who was soon in agreement with Harvey, that 'this lad Rooney' was an extraordinary player.

In the quarter-final against Nottingham Forest he notched the winner in a narrow 2–1 victory.

Then they met Tottenham Hotspur in a two-legged semi-final and Wayne scored twice in the second leg at Goodison, to put Everton into the final. It was this performance that really made people sit up and notice him. David Moyes was now the manager and watched his performance. He was quoted in James Corbett's book *Faith of Our Families: Everton FC, an Oral History*:

> I was in the gantry looking down and Wayne was stunning. I walked down, this would probably be about April time, and the boys had come back on the pitch for a cool down. I remember going up and tapping him on the shoulder and saying 'You'll be with me next year'. I didn't know him.

Glenn Hoddle, who was then managing Spurs, was equally impressed by the youngster's performance against his team and made an enquiry about his availability. Liverpool were still monitoring his progress, annoyed that they had not snapped him up when they had him on the premises for the trial. They always saw him as a genuine presence.

David Unsworth, who was to manage Rooney albeit briefly, was alerted also about the huge talent that was coming up fast through the ranks. John Murtagh was a long-serving member of the Everton backroom staff and had been watching Wayne progress since he was in the Under-10s. He was a pal of Unsworth and showed him a video recording of Wayne's goals in the semi-final. Unsworth, the man the fans called 'Rhino', was gobsmacked by what he saw and could only shake his head, muttering, 'Who the hell is that?'

Everton were hot favourites to beat Aston Villa, even though the latter were a strong team, including central defender Liam Ridgewell, skipper Stefan Moore, his younger brother striker Luke and midfielder Steven Davis. The quartet were all to go on to make an impact in the Premier. They shocked Everton by beating them 4–1 at Goodison Park in front of a partisan crowd of 15,000.

Wayne gave them a great start, firing home after twenty-five minutes. Celebrating wildly, he lifted his Everton shirt to reveal a white T-shirt with 'Once a blue, always a blue!' emblazoned on it (being the mantra by which he lived his life). And it is as relevant and as important to him today as it was back then.

The T-shirt had been customised by his cousin Toni, in the same way that John Lydon had ripped up his T-shirt, scrawled 'I hate Pink Floyd' across it, and stuck some safety pins through it. In this way, punk was born, as was similarly, Wayne Rooney's Everton career. A resonant image was formed and can be seen in his celebrations for goals scored in his comeback. It was a political statement, a statement of intent, indeed a declaration of love. In the same way, Pep Guardiola wore the yellow ribbons on his Man City training top: this was a personal statement to link him with the separatist movement in Catalonia.

Once a blue, always a blue!

It would be nice to say that Wayne's goal was the winner and he went on to win his first significant trophy for the Toffees. Aston Villa had other ideas though, for they outmuscled the young Toffees and went on to score four goals. Mr Moore's little boys, Stefan and Luke, were taking control and running riot. Wayne was stunned. It was his first major setback in his fledging football life. Before then he had swept everything before him, running riot and scoring freely.

Once again the parallels with Jimmy Greaves appear. For the opening six years of the FA Youth Cup the competition was won by Manchester United rather in the same fashion that Real Madrid had a stranglehold over the European Cup. The United domination was down to the nucleus of the brilliant 'Busby Babes', the men who were so tragically destroyed in the Munich air crash.

However, in 1957/58 though the monopoly was broken when Wolverhampton contested the final against Greaves's young Chelsea side, and the mercurial David Cliss was also in the team. The first leg played at Stamford Bridge went to Chelsea, who cruised to a 5–1 victory with young Jimmy scoring and dominating play. The young Chelsea lions thought that they only had to turn up for the second leg at Wolverhampton to lift the trophy.

Over 50,000 fans sardine-canned into Molyneux that night and saw an awesome display by the home side, who won 6–1 to take the Cup 7–6 on aggregate. Two years later, Chelsea won the FA Youth Cup with a side that included Terry Venables, Bobby Tambling and Peter Bonetti. The following year, they retained it with a fine win over a very talented Everton Youth team that included Colin Harvey.

Wayne was determined to turn things around in the second leg to be played at Villa Park, four days after the home debacle. The game became almost a personal duel between him and the Villa goalkeeper, Wayne Henderson. The young keeper literally stopped everything that Wayne threw at him as the striker shot from every conceivable angle.

Henderson gave a masterclass in the art of shot-stopping, although strangely he never played for Villa's first team, even though the Republic of Ireland capped him six times. The almost demented ambition and focus of Rooney drove him on and he could have scored a hat-trick but for the brilliance of the Villa custodian. Another rasping drive struck the crossbar but the only goal of the game was scored by Everton's Scott Brown. This followed a rare mistake by Liam Ridgewell, another player who went on to have a lengthy career in the Premier before joining Portland Timbers in the MLS (America's Major League Soccer).

The loss of the FA Youth Cup was a salutary lesson, for the naivety of youth had led Wayne to believe that they could simply carry on destroying teams. The defeat to Villa in his first real acid test made him realise that the Toffees were not even the best youth team in the land. Like all key lessons in life, it had been learnt the hard way. Skill and great fitness were only part of the footballer's craft, and mental toughness also had a great bearing on a successful player. For his age Wayne was so strong physically he could solve most problems that way. It had crossed his mind though, that as he went up levels, he would have to cultivate his 'game intelligence'.

Wayne might have been feeling pangs of insecurity as he returned to the dressing room. He slumped on the bench, too tired to change. All around him were his beaten teammates, exhausted by their efforts and downcast by defeat. Suddenly the Everton manager David Moyes strolled in, hands in his tracksuit pockets, a smile on his face. He came over to Wayne, obviously recalling their conversation after the Spurs semi-final.

'Tough luck out there tonight, Wayne,' he said. Our hero nodded back, and Moyes consoled him by saying what a good season he had enjoyed. At the end of the conversation he motioned to the outside corridor, saying, 'Have a word?'

Wayne wondered what he wanted: he knew 'goodbye' when he heard it. Perhaps that was the end of his career at Everton, the youth team of which he was the undoubted star, yet had proved to be found wanting when the crunch came.

He could not have been more wrong.

Moyes told him in confidence that next season he would be training with the first team: Wayne was moving on up.

CHAPTER 7

THE WALKING DEAD

'Maybe he is not a striker anymore but he will
never be a Number Six for me, he will never be
someone playing sixty metres from the goal.'
José Mourinho, on Rooney

EARLY AUTUMN 2017

Following the bad beating inflicted by Tottenham,
Everton headed out to Italy as they opened their Europa
League campaign. They were hoping to have a run in the
competition, not only to keep the money pot brimming but
to give much needed experience to their younger players.
Their most experienced player, Wayne, was relishing
the prospect of playing in Europe again, particularly in
a competition that he had won the previous season with
Manchester United.

The Toffees had qualified for the competition by beating

the Croatian side Hajduk Split in the playoffs. The first leg was played at Goodison Park and resulted in an edgy 2–0 home victory. The opening goal came from Michael Kane, heading in a deep cross from Leighton Baines on the half hour, his first for the club following his transfer from Burnley. Idrissa Gueye scored the second just before the break. The game was notable for the introduction at half-time of their new signing costing £45 million: Gylfi Sigurdsson, the Icelandic international from Swansea.

Some fans doubted the purchase of another Number 10 because they claimed he would merely duplicate the role that Wayne was currently occupying on the left side of midfield for Koeman. Add Davy Klaassen to the mix, but where was the new striker? José Mourinho had chopped and changed Wayne in the last few months of his time at Old Trafford. Mourinho wanted to use him primarily as a striker, but with Rooney's superpowers dwindling, he had pushed him deeper. Everton lacked pace and imagination in midfield and the use of him in that area meant that it was even more congested. Also, the likes of Sigurdsson would see less of the ball.

Sigurdsson scored an amazing fifty-yard goal in the return match in Croatia to earn Everton a 1–1 draw. Wayne played in the match and was one of the first players to congratulate Gylfi on his stupendous goal – he liked players who would try anything a bit different in a match. In March 2014, playing for Manchester United (then managed by David Moyes), he had hit a screamer from a distance, officially recorded as 57.9 yards, to score against West Ham. The likelihood of repeating such a trick again in a Premier match was exceedingly unlikely.

Ronald Koeman was bullish about the trip to Atalanta and was very pleased with Rooney's contribution to the team so far. He told the *Metro*: 'Rooney is a great player and has shown it from the start of the season. He is part of the team tomorrow and he travelled and is looking forward to the competition.'

As it happened Wayne's dreams of leading Everton to European glory turned into a nightmare as Atalanta tore them apart in the first half with some mesmerising football. Although only thirteenth in Serie A, way behind leaders Napoli, the Italians had too much class and won 3–0. The game was played at Sassuolo, 120 miles from Atalanta's home stadium, which was in the process of being refurbished. But Atalanta seemed completely at ease in their new environment as they enjoyed their first taste of European glory in twenty-six years.

After twenty-seven minutes Wayne dropped back to help his team defend a corner. He could only watch helplessly as the ball spun off defender Phil Jagielka and fell at the feet of Andrea Masiello, who merely had to tap it home.

The 2,500 Everton fans who had made the long trek could only watch in horror as Alejandro Gómez shrugged off a weak challenge from Nikola Vlašić, cut inside and curled home the second. Andrea Petagna and the Italian's midfield generalissimos were dominating the game and just on half-time, set up the third for Cristante.

Wayne trudged off at half-time, wiping his eyes on the

sixties spacesuit silver shirt with the made-up-sounding sponsor's name. There were no more goals in the second half but the relentless Italians continued to pummel the Merseyside team. It was a bad night for Wayne, and his teammates. Now serious questions were being asked about Koeman.

There was no respite for Wayne back home. He was paying a heavy price for his night out. The tabloids were holding his personal life up to scrutiny and examining it very closely. *The Sun* highlighted Wayne's night life and Coleen's holidays. By all accounts she was still furious with her husband. Meanwhile, his court appearance was scheduled for the following Monday. First, though, there was the little matter of a return to Manchester United and a clash with José Mourinho. Old Trafford was never a happy hunting ground for the Toffees, who had won there just twice since the Premier League era.

It was a bad time to be going back to his old stomping ground, though he had the bit between his teeth. United were unbeaten with Romelu Lukaku up front, and he had scored six goals in his last four games.

Mourinho was in fine form, pleased at his team's unbeaten start. After his humiliating exit from Chelsea, the Portuguese man cut a dishevelled figure, for once apparently lacking his great self-assurance, and often wearing trainers and less formal attire. Now he had his mojo back and was frequently clad in an expensive, beautifully-cut dark suit, crafted for him by the finest tailors in Milan, who were still grateful to him for coaching Inter Milan to the Champions League. The 'Special One' looked very businesslike, resembling someone from the legal profession or the upper echelons of Euro banking.

He spoke eloquently to the *Daily Mail* about Wayne's return, saying: 'I think he will get the welcome he deserves. Sometimes the word "legend" comes too easily. That is not the case here. The stadium will show him the respect he deserves – I hope before and after the match, not during the match.'

Whilst he was at Chelsea in his second term Mourinho had spent many hours plotting a possible transfer from Manchester United. Roman Abramovich never wanted Rooney playing for Chelsea. The tension came to a head in the third match of the season, where the clubs clashed at Old Trafford, and the West London side played without a striker until Torres came on late in the game. According to a member of the Chelsea staff, Mourinho's line-up was a challenge to the indifference that the Russian had shown to Mourinho's pleas to sign Rooney.

Fans in the Stretford End of the stand sang his name after the pre-match warm-up as he walked off the field arm-in-arm with Michael Carrick. It was said that Rooney was 'admired' by the United crowd but not 'adored'. It was different at Everton, where he was loved because he was more readily identifiable.

Rooney's goals record for Manchester United looks unbeatable because goals are harder to score these days than when Wayne was at his peak. Before he left United he had broken Sir Bobby Charlton's club record and set a new mark of 253 goals. Now he was keen to score against

United and, in turn, become the eighth ex-United player to accomplish such a feat.

But there was no happy return to the Theatre of Dreams for Wayne, as they went down 0–4. The scoreline was a bit harsh on Everton but they never recovered from going behind to an early goal from Antonio Valencia. Wayne tried to spearhead an Everton revival but his only clear-cut chance was saved by De Gea, using his legs. Being the lone striker in Koeman's unambitious 5–4–1 line-up was a thankless task.

Wayne eventually became tired and was taken off towards the end, to be replaced by Kevin Mirallas. The stats indicated that he had made seventy-two touches of the ball during the eighty-two minutes he had played. (At his peak, on average his feet touched the ball ninety times in one game and he ran 11.82 km.) As he made his way off the pitch the whole ground rose as one to acclaim him. He was like a gladiator leaving the arena he had dominated for so long.

That seemed to trigger a late collapse. Romelu Lukaku set up Henrikh Mkhitaryan for United's second goal, then smashed in a third. For long periods of the game Wayne had looked in better form than the Belgian, who missed an easy first-half chance. A last-minute penalty from Anthony Martial sealed it for United and gave a false impression of their superiority.

The rot was setting in for Everton, because that was the sixth game in a row that they had failed to win. They had lost the last four without finding the net. In fact, the only League goals they had scored were both Rooney's.

Mourinho, forever the master of spin and propaganda, used his programme notes as a Machiavellian manifesto. In that day's edition he made a point about Everton's £140-million outlay in the last transfer window. His inference was that they would be aiming for, 'At least the top four.'

The 'Special One' was a little off-kilter with his maths, as the net spend was nearer to £50 million once the fee they had received from United for Lukaku had been factored in. Mourinho had little affection for Koeman, as he was one of the Barca players that scathingly referred to him as 'The Translator'. This was a disparaging reference to the fact that he had been employed by their club for his skills as a translator for Bobby Robson, rather than as a coach.

Everton tumbled into the bottom three on goal difference. It was perhaps the wrong day for the Toffees to unveil their new sleeve sponsors: Angry Birds (a video game). The club had entered into a deal with the Finnish company Rovio Entertainment, the game's developers. Angry Birds had a global brand awareness third only to Disney and Logo. It was a shrewd move by the club's commercial department. It was estimated that the Angry Birds game had achieved 3.75 billion downloads since 2009, 3 billion YouTube views, and gathered 25 million followers on Facebook.

The firm had a history of Angry Bird homages to real-life characters and speculation was rife that potentially Wayne Rooney would be involved. Can you imagine that, Wayne immortalised in a game? The main character in the game was red and his name also happened to be Red, so immediately there was controversy over the conflict between the 'blue' and the 'red' clubs of Merseyside. Red was also the colour of other hated enemies such as Manchester United and Arsenal.

Speaking of Angry Birds, Wayne appeared the next day at Stockport Magistrates Court, where he was banned from the roads for two years and ordered to perform one hundred hours of unpaid work. This was part of a twelve-month community order. For the occasion he was clad in what appeared to be a Boss two-button navy-blue suit, pristine white Egyptian cotton shirt, blue-on-blue dotted tie and black, spit-polished, Russell & Bromley shoes with buckles.

His solicitor Michael Rainford told the court:

> Wayne wishes to express his genuine remorse for what was a terrible mistake, a terrible error of judgement on his part that evening. He realises he has not only let himself down very badly but his family.
>
> He has a wife and three young children. Of course, he has let down the fans, the young people who look [up to] him.

The results of the breath test indicated a reading of 104 micrograms of alcohol per 100 millilitres of breath. The legal limit for England is thirty-five. The Everton striker was ordered to pay court costs of £170. In his summing up the District judge, John Temperley, told the former England captain: 'I am aware of the adverse effects that this has had on you but perhaps more importantly on your family. I am not convinced that a high level of fine would have the same punitive effect as a community order would.'

Rooney told the *Metro*: 'My actions were completely wrong. I want to apologise to all the fans and everyone else who has followed and supported me. I accept the sentence of the court and hope that I can make some amends through my community service.'

The Sun ran a headline 'Wayne Broomy', using one of those caricatures with his head superimposed onto a small body. Paddy Power, the bookmakers, were using a lot of those head shots in their adverts for football betting. For instance, there'd be a little figure of Wayne in an Everton shirt, with captions such as: first goal scorer, anytime scorer, untold odds if he scored a hat-trick, etc., etc.

The tabloids also carried pictures of Ms Laura Simpson arriving for work that day in her trusty old black Volkswagen. Later in the week they carried reports of her losing her mobile phone. Laura, meanwhile, tweeted 'Can't find my phone... took the keypad [lock] off it too ffs... game over if it's lost'. She claimed that she had mislaid the phone following a night out in the Rosso Restaurant, whose proprietor happened to be Wayne's former England and United teammate Rio Ferdinand.

Coleen's answer to all this was to take the kids away on half-term holiday to the exclusive Sandy Lane resort in Barbados. But with Everton rooted in the bottom three, there was no way their star striker could take the time off to join them.

Now Wayne was given a lift to training every morning

in a black top-of-the range Range Rover. The ninety-mile round trip from Cheshire to the club's Finch Farm training complex was a chore. Wayne usually sat in the front seat, dark baseball cap pulled down low, watching the countryside flash by, seemingly just an ordinary bod going to work. The Everton striker was a great Harry Potter fan and had read all of JK Rowling's oeuvre but did not take the opportunity of catching up on his reading during these drives.

The next fixture was a home tie in what was now known as the Carabao Cup. Some of us remember this event when it was originally known as the League Cup, and later the Milk Cup. Their opponents were Sunderland, relegated last season and in freefall. Ronald Koeman saw it as a chance to arrest the slide. In the end Everton ran out easy winners 3–0. Wayne was not amongst the scorers, two of them going to the rookie Dominic Calvert-Lewin, their leggy purchase from Sheffield Utd.

Dominic was seen as a prospect. He was very raw but had potential and with someone such as Wayne Rooney alongside him he could only improve. It was a bit like a *Strictly Come Dancing* contestant having tango lessons from Fred Astaire. The young pup Calvert-Lewin scored in the thirty-ninth and fifty-first minutes and Niasse wrapped it up in the closing ones. The Toffees' reward was a trip away to Chelsea. Thanks a lot!

Everton were at home again a few days later against Bournemouth. Koeman was anxious about this game. It was a must-win against a team that had done well to survive in the Premier and its unequal distribution of wealth. Their manager, Eddie Howe, was a boyhood Everton fan and a great admirer of Wayne, and he told the *Metro*: 'He's an outstanding player. I've always been one of his biggest fans. From United to England, there's no doubt he's one of the best goal scorers of his generation. He will be a real threat technically and he'll make them play, but he has lost none of his finishing ability.'

After forty-nine minutes, Josh King opened the scoring for Bournemouth with a fine finish after seizing on a pass from Charlie Daniels. The pressure was cranked up on the Dutch manager as Everton appeared to be heading for their fifth successive Premier League defeat without scoring. Only a wonderful save from Jordan Pickford kept his side in the match when he kept out a fierce drive from the veteran striker Jermaine Defoe. The cut-one-and-we-all-bleed camaraderie of Bournemouth made them hard to break down.

Wayne was huffing and puffing in a vain attempt to get Everton moving. He had precious little support and nobody to put the shovel work in up front. It came as no surprise when he was substituted along with Davy Klaassen soon afterwards. Niasse came onto the field – he was the forgotten man of Everton, signed from Lokomotiv Moscow for £13.5 million. He was ostracised by Koeman, who saw him as a busted flush and had him training with the Academy side. Subsequently, he was shipped out to Hull for the remainder of the season as they slid out of the Premier. But the Senegal striker's rehabilitation started on seventy-seven minutes in, when he latched on a through ball from his fellow sub Davies to thump home the equaliser. Five minutes later, the duo combined to set up the winner, Davy's shot was blocked, and Oumar (Niasse) hooked in the winner to grab three precious points.

After the match Koeman insisted that suggestions that he was under pressure were ridiculous. Comparisons were being drawn with a calamitous period he had as manager of Spanish team Valencia in a woeful six-month period in 2008. The ex-Barca star spoke of the open relationship he had with his players and stated that he had no reason to doubt his connection with them. He made particular reference to the senior stars that were old enough and experienced enough to understand what was key. Things were to deteriorate even further for him though, as Burnley beat them 1–0 at Goodison on the last day of September. Koeman gambled by dropping Wayne down to the bench and starting with the youthful zest of Dominic Calvert-Lewin and Nikola Vlašić. Last week's hero, Oumar Niasse, started the game. Wayne had been struggling in the last few matches: playing in a team without pace had exposed the fact that he had lost his own.

Speaking about his decision to bench Wayne, the Everton manager told the *Daily Mail*, 'He is committed to the team and to every Evertonian and he showed that. I explained the situation, that we changed the style of play. Like every professional player he accepted it.'

Burnley had not won at Everton since January 1976 and at the end of the game a torrent of boos greeted the final whistle. The only goal of the game came after twenty-one minutes, when Jeff Hendrick skipped past Morgan

Schneiderlin to finish off a slick passing move. Last season Schneiderlin had been an assault tank in midfield but this year...

Wayne was brought on after sixty-three minutes for Schneiderlin and sparked a series of attacks. The Everton substitute produced one of the only two shots on target all game. In the closing minutes Wayne melodramatically protested that he should have had a penalty when he flicked on Sigurdsson's cut-back cross and it bounced onto Matthew Lowton's arm. No penalty was granted despite his protestations.

The *Match of the Day* pundit Danny Murphy analysed Wayne's contribution later that day and talked of his 'Courage on the ball'.

After the game the press mobbed Ronald Koeman, like sharks smelling blood. He snapped at a journalist who enquired if he was still the right man for the club. The usual old clichés were wheeled out about Rooney waning. There was little doubt though that the Merseysiders were in crisis. The *Daily Mail*'s Chris Sutton predicted that Koeman's days at Everton were numbered. The storm clouds were gathering but it was to get worse before it got better.

CHAPTER 8

YOUTHQUAKE

'I believe Moyes was clever to treat a player like Rooney as he did, because Wayne started training with us in pre-season, so we always had the sensation he was a great player. We knew that. We knew he was going to be a top player. But he did well, the manager, to let him play not every game. He gave him the time to grow by himself, not to try to rush him.'

ALESSANDRO PISTONE, EVERTON PLAYER 2000–05

AUGUST 2002

Season 2002/3 commenced with Wayne training with the first team following his fast tracking there by the excited coaching staff. To most of them his talent was not comprehensible on any level. The famed Everton Academy had been the incubator for multiple stars but not one like this – a player who was so ahead of the curve.

In his first training session David Unsworth tried to 'initiate' him with a crunching tackle but Wayne dodged the full impact and a few minutes later nutmegged him. For a first-team player to be humiliated in such a fashion by what he considered to be an absolute beginner was humiliating. Even more so when he cruised past him shortly afterwards to score with a low drive. As a player Unsworth was good-hearted and hard, but as a first-team coach and an interim manager he struggled. The media made the unarguable conclusion that he was not up to operating at that level. The paths of the men they called 'Rhino' and 'Wayne' were to intersect again in the coming years.

Wayne had taken over Paul Gascoigne's shirt, Number 18. Paul John Gascoigne was born in Tyne and Wear but was named after two of Liverpool's most famous sons: John Lennon and Paul McCartney. Nicknamed 'Gazza', he was hailed the greatest player of his generation. His was a truly wonderful talent with great technique and a brilliant football brain but he was also a maniacal boozer. By the time he was winding down his career at Everton his sublime talent was gradually crushed by serious injury and life's hard knocks. It could be said that his ruinous lifestyle had caught up with him finally, as the drink began to take its toll.

The Gazza that Everton fans saw was a pale shell of the player who had exploded on the scene with Newcastle. Walter Smith, who had managed him at Rangers, had signed Gascoigne on a free transfer from Middleborough as a gamble.

After a bright start, the ongoing depression and niggling

injuries cost him a first-team place. He ended up in Arizona in rehab as his vulnerable psyche succumbed, but the following season, 2001/02, he briefly battled back. With consummate ease he scored the winner away to Bolton, which was the only goal he scored for the Toffees. Sadly, it was also his last in the big time, a poignant end for a player felt by many to have been the equal, or indeed superior, to any Englishman before or after him. A hernia operation and the dismissal of Walter Smith brought an end to his brief career at Everton.

Tony Hibbert, who did a great deal to help Wayne in his early days, is on record as saying that Gazza was 'the nicest fella' he ever met in football. The former England superstar departed to Burnley, where he played a handful of games before his career tapered off.

Wayne used to see him sometimes at Bellefield, sitting in the physio's room. On one occasion he was in floods of tears. Weeks later, he found out that the Geordie icon was upset because he had assisted in laying on a winning goal against his beloved 'black and whites'. Even back then his life was unravelling, his unhappiness spilling over into everything. Soon it fizzled and dissipated.

Kitman Jimmy Martin would keep Wayne amused with cartoonish Gazza stories. His favourite was about the time Gazza sent his major domo, Jimmy 'Five Bellies', Gardner out to buy fifteen kettles (the boil-up 'whistling' variety, with a removable end for filling). He chucked away the kettles and stuck the removable ends – fashioned to make a whistling sound by escaping bubbling water vapour – onto the exhausts of the players' cars. You should have heard the noise when they drove away after training. Gazza and his pal Jimmy just sat on the wall, pissing themselves with laughter.

The Geordie's bleak descent into alcoholism is one of the saddest stories of recent times. If Gascoigne was the best of his generation then it would be fair to say that Wayne Rooney was the most gifted of his. Just imagine if the two biggest hitters of their generations could have both played for England together at their peak?

It would be fair to say that neither absolutely fulfilled their promise of being world-beaters but they came very close. To think of how close is to weep for the modern game and the fact that, despite the self-justificatory and hyperbolic praise heaped on certain players, no Englishman has stepped up to the plate.

The current England squad does not have another Gascoigne or Rooney to make things happen. Gazza and Roo, as the media tagged them, were the football equivalents of shooting stars across the vast backdrop of the domestic and international game. Both men were persons of interest for as long as they could remember, followed and photographed by the press and judged for every move and every comment. Their lives were never their own and in today's world of social media they never will be.

Wayne survived for two reasons: the love of a good wife and his unique bond with Everton Football Club. Wayne Rooney had been many different things in his time on earth but he was always an Evertonian. As a young player at Goodison he put armour on and created his own legend.

Gazza was not so lucky; he retreated into a drink-assisted mourning for his past life and career. The most fabulously notorious footballer of his age. Joey Barton was another product of the Everton Youth Academy and a tough upbringing in Liverpool. Joey Barton ran Gazza close in the 'mayhem stakes'. Although Barton was a good player, he was not in the same class. Gascoigne at his best was unstoppable; his audacious goal in the Euro 1996 campaign against Scotland is proof of that. The problem was he never learnt.

One of the reasons that Wayne made it through was the fantastic amount of work he put in. Jimmy Martin would tell stories of how after training he would go into the kit room and ask him for a bag of balls. He would then go back onto the pitch and spend the rest of the afternoon belting the balls into goal, hour after hour. Firing in shots from more angles than a Russian protractor. Always looking for the edge, the perfect volley, the trick shot that landed the killer blow. A genius allied to drive.

Wayne made his first team debut as a brilliantly precious sixteen-year-old for Everton against Tottenham Hotspur at Goodison Park on 17 August 2002 in front of a crowd of 40,120. He was in the team on merit, having scored nine goals in the pre-season friendlies. In a friendly against Hibs he was taken off early after a running battle with one of their defenders.

Wayne stayed out of trouble on his debut, though some of the Spurs defenders did try and intimidate him. He did not realise at first how much talking/sledging went on in a game. One particular Tottenham defender spent a great deal of time badmouthing him and questioning his parentage and his presence in the team.

It may be of interest to note the teams on that hot summer's afternoon were:

Everton (4–4–2)
Wright, Hibbert, Weir, Stubbs, Naysmith,
Graveson, Li Tie (Substitute Redrigo 76),
Pembridge, Radzinski (Substitute Unsworth 84),
Campbell, Rooney (Substitute Alexanderson 66)
Tottenham Hotspur (4–4–2)
Keller, Carr (Substitute Thatcher 44), Richards,
Gardner, Tarnico, Davies, Redknapp, Bunjevcević,
Etherington, Sheringham, (Captain, Substitute
Ferdinand 71), Iversen.

It was a strong Spurs team which included the England International Teddy Sheringham, a treble winner with Manchester United, and Jamie Redknapp, now a respected TV pundit. Redknapp, making his debut that day following his move from Liverpool, was no stranger to the tabloid headlines himself. At around the time Wayne returned to Everton, Jamie's high-profile marriage to ex-Eternal pop star Louise was disintegrating. Incidentally, in his autobiography Wayne nominated Jamie as his favourite pundit.

Over the years Spurs had become something of a bogey side to Everton, for they had beaten the side from North London just once in twenty Premiership matches. There was a carnival atmosphere in the air, and the first game of a new season was always a time for optimism, renewed hope and fresh faces to cheer. Everton had a new goalkeeper, having invested £3.5 million in Richard Wright and £5 million on the Nigerian Joseph Yobo. All eyes were on Wayne, who at sixteen years and 298 days was the youngest player to feature in the Premier League. Not the youngest ever to play for Everton though. That honour went to Joe Royle, who beat Wayne by two weeks. Joe was in the crowd that day as Everton were celebrating one hundred years of top-class football. Many old faces were invited, including Duncan McKenzie, Derek Temple, Alex Young and Bob Latchford. Little did they know but they were witnessing the birth of another legend. There were few regrets in his life but Wayne was always disappointed that he did not get the record for the youngest ever Everton player.

The Spurs fans noticed him too, because his exploits had been observed down south. Their manager Glenn Hoddle was a big fan and the cockneys greeted him with the familiar refrain of: 'Who are ya? Who are ya?'

Soon everyone was to know exactly who he was.

Wayne did not score but had an impressive debut, featuring in a three-pronged attack with the ex-Arsenal striker Kevin Campbell and the Pole Tomasz Radzinski. The high spot in his performance was when he made a goal for Mark Pembridge. Back then the term 'assist' was not in vogue, but his action most definitely fell into that category. It was a neat clipped pass, putting the midfielder in for the first goal of the game, after Radzinksi fed Wayne. The move had started when Tarrico over-committed in midfield and

Radzinski raced away down the right. Pembridge, a man from Wales, was the first to congratulate the youngster on his part in scoring the goal.

The Welshman was a real character, the life and soul of the dressing room, always pulling stunts and cracking jokes. It was he who had christened Wayne 'Dog', a sobriquet which was to stick throughout the duration of his first stint at Everton. The origins of it were obscure; some say it was because he was compared to a Rottweiler because of his tenacity and combative manner. Another crueller possibility was because some thought he resembled a bulldog. Wayne insisted that it was because in his early days at the club he used to wear an Everton 'Dogs of War' T-shirt in homage to the Cup-winning side.

Tottenham equalised through Etherington on the hour from almost the same position Pembridge had scored. Wayne almost put Everton ahead but the American keeper Kasey Keller tipped his fierce drive over the bar. After seventy-seven minutes Moyes subbed his young hero with the teams level at 1–1. Wayne was most displeased because he could have run for hours and the close attention from the Tottenham rearguard were not, in his view, getting to him.

The Everton fans gave the player in the '18' shirt a terrific reception as he left the field. They loved nothing more than seeing a young player come through. When Walter Smith was in charge he had either sold or not used the youth team players that had won the FA Youth Cup. The Scot had gone for the quick fix and brought in the likes of Gazza (thirty-three), David Ginola (thirty-five), Mark Hughes (thirty-six) and Richard Gough (thirty-seven). It was a two-edged sword: youngsters like Wayne could learn from great players, but the practice also stopped the progression of longer-term players.

Perhaps Moyes thought to protect the youngster as he knew how combustible Wayne was. The last thing he wanted was to wrap the lad in cotton wool but he was aware of just how tough the Premier could be. Moyes would always tell the story of how he first drove into Liverpool he saw the kids playing football in the street. It reminded him of the old days in Glasgow but what struck him most was that everyone was wearing Everton shirts. It made him think that people on the streets supported Everton. Wayne Rooney was the epitome of that memory.

The game ended in a 2–2 draw and Les Ferdinand being substitute for Teddy put Spurs ahead after a mistake by Wright. Radzinski saved a point for the Toffees when he jinxed into the box to slot home the equaliser. Wayne, now back in the dugout, was on his feet cheering along with the rest of the euphoric crowd.

Orson Welles's observation about 'the confidence of ignorance' could be applied to this stage of Rooney's career. Wayne was far from ignorant of what lay ahead for him though. So far in all his short life he had been playing against opponents a lot older and in some cases stronger than himself. He always knew what was coming next as he surged past a defender: the lunge, the swinging boot, the raking of studs across the ankles. The kid from Croxteth could look after himself though.

On his debut he put a shuddering challenge in on the

Tottenham defender Steven Carr, who was forced to leave the game. Wayne was instantly ready for fame; he had the modesty of players who never doubted their own ability. Playing for Everton in the Premier League was the realisation of a long-held dream for him. Now he had another objective in his sights: to score his first goal in the big time.

Wayne's relationship with David Moyes oscillated somewhat. Now he was on his way to being a star and in turn a celebrity. For anyone this would have been bewildering, but for a sixteen-year-old from the backstreets of Liverpool? Imagine all the fame, glamour and attention; being a fixture in the newspapers and being whisked around in cars and jets. Anyone receiving such attention would think that it was about them personally, but really it was as a result of Everton making money from him.

All con tricks work on the basis of getting the victim or 'mark' to believe that attention they get is about them. Their ego will tell them that. For Wayne to have believed anything else at that stage would have been impossible. It was a brilliant time for him in every sense of the word. Brilliant in the sense that the cameras and TV lights were popping in his face, blinding him to what was actually happening.

Wayne did not feature in the next Premier game away to Sunderland, which they won by a solitary goal. Moyes had told him he would not be playing but he found it hard to accept, as he knew that he was so near a breakthrough.

He broke his cherry in a game against Wrexham of all teams on 1 October 2002 in the second round of the League Cup at the Racecourse Ground. Scoring twice after coming on as sub, Everton had gone in front through Kevin Campbell after twenty-five minutes. Wayne liked playing alongside Campbell. In recent times the leading sides just play with one up-top, but back then everyone played with two and whoever was in the Number 10 position was a proper 10. This suited Wayne perfectly, and it still does.

Everton were lucky to have signed an experienced striker like the ex-Arsenal centre-forward. He came on loan from the Turkish side Trabzonspor on deadline day, 1999. There had been some problems in Turkey, having been racially abused. Campbell was very versatile. In his early career at Arsenal he had played as an orthodox striker but when Ian Wright joined, he switched to a target man role. He formed a good partnership with Franny Jeffers, who would play off his shoulder. Wayne was following in Jeffers's footsteps and when he left to join Arsenal for £8 million a vacancy occurred.

Kevin Campbell was a very generous man. He was old school, believing, the older players should support and teach the younger ones the ropes. Campbell first took Jeffers, then another boy from a rough neighbourhood, Rooney, under his wing. It definitely made things easier for Wayne to make such a good impression at that stage. That is why it is so hard for young players today to break through the glass ceiling at the top clubs. Chelsea might be the best example of this and the reason why players such as Ruben Loftus-Cheek and Tammy Abraham found it easier to break into the England team than their own club's first team.

Campbell had first played alongside Wayne when he was fourteen in a friendly at Southport. He was feeling his way back after injury and was informed that this young kid who looked like an overgrown baby was going to be his strike partner. Shaking his head in disbelief, he asked Colin Harvey if he was sure. After only playing an hour, Kevin came off, still shaking his head in disbelief. Everton were leading 3–0, Rooney had scored twice and made the other for him.

The score was the same 3–0, and the scorers the same Campbell and two for Rooney. Wayne had come on for Radzinski and scored his first after eighty-three minutes. It was following a strong run and at the finish it was a bit lucky in that the ball went through the goalkeeper's legs. That put him in the record books as the youngest scorer in the history of Everton, at sixteen years, 342 days. It beat the record set in 1937 by Tommy Lawton, who was a mere strip of a lad of seventeen years and 130 days. (To digress slightly, Lawton had the record for the youngest player to score a League hat-trick: Burnley v Spurs. At the risk of sounding like the stats man on *Test Match Special* he was also the youngest player to score in a Merseyside derby.)

The second Rooney goal was a gem though, a mazy dribble and a strong finish. Those Everton fans who had made the trip were treated to a little piece of history but his next goal for Everton was, to be even more spectacular and would pass into folklore.

CHAPTER 9

BREAKING BAD

'We are afraid to play.'
RONALD KOEMAN, AFTER THE 2–2 HOME DRAW
WITH APOLLON LIMASSOL

OCTOBER 2017

Things became worse for Everton as the season changed from summer to autumn and their season rapidly turned into a collective malaise. Before they had lost at home to Burnley, Everton had a home tie against Apollon Limassol in the Europa League. The game had ended in a 2–2 draw – another hugely disappointing performance against one of the minnows of the competition. Apollon had lost each of their past five Europa League group matches they had played away from home. An eighty-eighth minute header from Hector Juste earned them an unlikely point. This goal came just 118 seconds after a red card had been shown to the visitors, to Valentin Roberge.

The only high spot in the match for Rooney was when he scored possibly the easiest goal of his long career. A misplaced pass from the goal-scorer Hector Juste gifted him the ball in the penalty area. All he had to do was literally walk the ball into the net. An error of equal stupidity had given the Cypriot team the lead when a shocking clearance from the out-of-form Ashley Williams had cost them a goal. Nikola Vlaši appeared to have scored the winner when the Croatian teenager raced onto Gylfi Sigurdsson's neat pass and tucked the ball home. It was a double first, Nikola's goal and Sigurdsson's assist, but Everton remained at the bottom of Group E.

Wayne told BT Sport: 'It is hard to take. We were the better team but the goals were sloppy from our point of view. There's no easy games in Europe. Some of the decisions this season we have not got, we are picking up injuries and knocks from not being protected enough.'

The next Premier game they had was away to newly promoted Brighton, managed by Chris Houghton, one of the shrewdest coaches in the business. The Toffees were win-less in their past twelve away games. This was their longest sequence since a run of thirteen games ending back in March 2002, shortly before Wayne had made his League debut. The Seagulls looked set to win after going ahead through Anthony Knockaert but a late penalty from Wayne gave them a point that they scarcely deserved. The penalty was awarded when their defender Bruno elbowed Dominic

Calvert-Lewin in the area as a free kick was floated over. Already a partnership was beginning to blossom between the two players which had echoes of Wayne's early days at Goodison Park and his combination with Kevin Campbell.

The penalty was dispatched easily by Wayne's right foot into the bottom left corner of the goal, after he had sent the Brighton keeper Mat Ryan the wrong way. Wayne was still a player who could strike fear into the best goalkeepers in Europe. His penalty technique was excellent, precise and cleverly executed. With the season well under way, he was still scoring top-flight goals, although sections of the press were writing his football obituary. Immediately after scoring the equaliser Wayne was replaced by Tom Davies.

The late penalty he had converted against Brighton meant that he had now scored against thirty-six of the thirty-nine different clubs he had faced in the Premier League. Only Frank Lampard (thirty-nine), Andrew Cole (thirty-eight) and Alan Shearer (thirty-seven) had scored against more sides in the competition. Jermaine Defoe, who he had played against recently in the narrow win over Bournemouth, was also on the thirty-six mark. The only sides that Wayne had failed to score against included Manchester United (as previously discussed, the 0–4 hammering in September 2017 was his fifth attempt). The other teams were Derby County and Blackpool (both two attempts). With Derby still trying to fight their way out of the Championship and Blackpool plummeting down the leagues, it is unlikely that he will ever get the chance to rectify that situation.

Then it was back to a Thursday night Europa League

Group home game against the classy Lyon. Everton desperately needed to win the match to have any chance of progressing in the competition. However, with a tough fixture against Arsenal on the following Sunday the under-pressure Koeman made five changes. Wayne watched another defeat from the comfort of a heated executive box. The side in blue went down 1–2 to their slick French opponents. Rooney's absence polarised opinions amongst the fans. It highlighted the parlous position that the Toffees found themselves in. Some agreed that survival in the Premier was the first priority, but what had happened to the Ronald Koeman doctrine of 'one game at a time'?

Apart from the incident involving the supporter from the Gwladys Street end cradling his infant and throwing punches, the most notable event was the brave fight put up by the Everton youngsters. The club legend that was Peter Reid had that very week accused the players of being unable 'to scrap'. That was far from the truth that night but they soon fell behind to Lyon after the French team's skipper, Fekir, scored from the penalty spot. The ex-Manchester United outcast Memphis Depay had engineered the move that led to the penalty being awarded when defender Mason Holgate chopped down Marçal. Koeman had tried to sign the Holland winger from United the previous season but had been unable to clinch the deal. Unshaven and badly stressed, Koeman looked at the ground as the penalty went in. That night he was fighting to save his job. It was the tenth time in the last eleven matches that Everton had conceded the first goal.

BREAKING BAD

Ashley Williams, who had sparked the melee with his fierce challenge on the Lyon keeper, equalised with a header from Sigurdsson's clever free kick. But the mobile Lyon side had the last word, with ex-Chelsea striker Traoré back-heeling the winner after seventy-five minutes. As the final whistle blew in a storm of booing, Wayne headed for home, head down, hands thrust deep into the pockets of his expensive overcoat. Koeman was on the brink of the sack, though he claimed that he still had the backing of the board. The bookmakers Paddy Power slashed the odds on him being the next Premier boss to being out of a job to 1–7 on.

Everton were unlucky to be drawn in the same group as a side as sophisticated as Lyon. It was already being called the 'group of death'. Pep Guardiola was an admirer of Lyon's attacking style and had sent his first-team coach and talent spotter Mikel Arteta to check them out. Mikel had spent six seasons at Goodison and nodded across to Wayne as he took his seat nearby. It was a testimony to the growing reputation of the Lyon team that they were being monitored by the game's elite. The fact remained though that Everton had made the worst-ever start of an English team in the competition and the vultures were hovering.

Mike Parry, the talkSPORT commentator, was always a staunch Evertonian and a huge Wayne Rooney fan. He even wrote a book about him, the amusingly titled '*Rooney Tunes*'. On his radio show, *The Two Mikes*, he spoke of the Dutchman's aloofness. Of how he always ate first at the canteen before the players arrived, and how he exuded a cold manner with those he dealt with. Rumours were rife as to who would replace him. David Moyes was linked, along with the Watford coach Marco Silva, Burnley's Sean Dyche and the former England manager Sam Allardyce. *Very superstitious...Writing on the wall* Stevie Wonder once sang. The writing was on the wall all right for Ronald Koeman.

Speaking of beleaguered managers, Arsène Wenger, the one who had racked up the most wins against Everton (thirty), was heading to Goodison. It happened to be his sixty-eighth birthday, and also Arsenal had problems of their own that Sunday afternoon, namely a schizoid team capable of out-footballing any side in Europe, yet defensively weak. Their two truly world-class players, Alexis Sánchez and Mesut Özil, had run down their contracts and the word was that both were in their last season with the club. It was unlucky for Everton and particularly Koeman that when the duo played that afternoon they were joined by their £52.7-million record signing Alexandre Lacazette. It was the first time that the trio had played together.

The game could not have started better for Wayne when he opened the scoring after twelve minutes. On the night he had been tested against Lyon it had been exactly fifteen years since he had announced himself with his sumptuous match-winning first league goal against Arsenal (more of that in the next chapter). The latest Rooney goal was scored at the same end of the ground and hit with a similar destructive suddenness. It was fitting that Wayne should summon up his immense talents to conjure a replica of one of his greatest ever goals. That superb goal gave him twelve in the Premier League against Arsenal, more than any other player in the history of the competition.

In an attempt to re-live his glory days Wayne was wearing retro boots. Two goals had been struck using his Nike Total 90 Laser 11s: the penalty down at Brighton and his effort that day. The Arsenal keeper Petr Čech, who had been so comprehensively beaten that afternoon, had been in goal for Chelsea in the 2008 Champions League Final. The last time Wayne had worn Nike Total 90 Laser 11s was in that match.

The game was being covered on Radio 5 live and commentator Steve Claridge was in raptures about the strike, saying he was, 'Still doing it.'

Mike Parry on talkSPORT that evening described it as a, 'Sublime goal by Rooney.'

It would have been nice for the prodigal son's sentimental goal to have settled the match but there was to be no fairy-tale, ending that day. New York may have had their fairy tales especially around Christmas time, but there were none on Merseyside. Wenger's Arsenal were a reactive team and, stung by Rooney's excellent goal, proceeded to tear into Everton. The mobility and movement of Lacazette stretched the home side's defence to near breaking point and created space for Mesut Özil and Sánchez to cause havoc. Only a string of brilliant saves by Jordan Pickford kept them out, and one particular save from Granit Xhaka's blockbuster of a shot was outstanding. Just when it looked like Everton might hang on until half-time, wing-back Nacho Monreal hammered home a rebound to equalise. Wayne left the field shaking his head, fearing for the rest of the game and knowing that Everton had a mountain to climb.

The second half was a slaughterhouse as Arsenal put Everton to the sword. Man of the Match Mesut Özil put Arsenal in front with a rare headed goal from a cross by Sánchez. Things could only get worse and Idrissa Gueye was sent off following a second yellow card after a reckless foul on Xhaka. Wayne protested in vain as Everton went down to ten men. Shortly afterwards Sánchez fed Özil, who carved out a chance for Lacazette to make it 3–1. This sparked a huge exodus of Everton fans, who knew that the game was now over as a contest. Wayne was substituted at this point. He glared across at Koeman as he departed, and there was a late flurry of goals in the closing minutes and stoppage time. Aaron Ramsey scored Arsenal's fourth after a fine pass from Jack Wilshere, slowly rehabilitating himself after a nightmare run of injuries.

Everton substitute Oumar Niasse scored a late consolation after Čech and Monreal got into a muddle. With literally the last kick of the match, Sánchez made it 5–2 with a fierce shot past the shell-shocked Pickford. Arsenal had now scored one hundred Premier League goals against Everton – the first instance of a club scoring a ton against a single opponent. It was always an amazing fixture when those two tangled. It gave Arsenal their first away win of the season but Everton were now in meltdown, sitting eighteenth in the Premier, having won just two of their first nine games. Add to that the fact that they were facing their own version of

Brexit. The attacks in the press on Koeman's management style intensified and the switchboards on the phone-ins were jammed with irate Evertonians.

The inevitable happened to Ronald Koeman, just as the jubilant Arsenal away contingent had predicted, saying, 'You're getting sacked in the morning.'

On Monday morning a club statement read: 'Chairman Bill Kenwright, the board of directors and major shareholder Farhad Moshiri would all like to express their gratitude to Ronald for the service he has given to the club over the past sixteen months and for guiding the club to seventh place in last year's Premier League.'

The dumped Dutchman replied on Twitter: 'I would like to place on record my thanks to the players and staff for all their work. Naturally I am disappointed but I wish the team good luck in the future.'

David Unsworth, the Under-23s boss, stepped into an interim role for the second time in eighteen months. He had stepped up to the breach when Roberto Martínez was sacked. The forty-four-year-old announced that he was keen to secure the role full-time.

But where did this leave our protagonist? The dream return to his boyhood club now looked in danger of turning sour. His career was hanging by a thread.

CHAPTER 10

OH, WHAT A PERFECT DAY

'There's only a couple of times when I've left Goodison, when you're in the changing room and you can hear the crowd a little bit going out. There's probably only two or three occasions where it was rapturous down the whole street, everybody. That was one of the days, because of the result and the introduction of Wayne. He was one of their own – probably half of the supporters might have known Wayne from playing in the streets with him, bumping into him or going to school with him. I think when it's like that and you know somebody who's so good and has scored that goal. I think it means an awful lot to people.'

DAVID MOYES

OCTOBER 2002

Lou Reed sang of 'a perfect day'. For readers of a different generation you may recall Matt Monro crooning at the start of the film *The Italian Job* about 'Days like this'. Wayne's goal against Arsenal made the perfect day for many people on Merseyside on 19 October 2002. Of course it was not such a perfect day if you were an Arsenal fan. They had put together a run of thirty-one games unbeaten and were looking to extend it. Goodison Park, as we have seen, was a happy hunting ground for Arsenal Football Club.

Since his two-goal performance at Wrexham, Moyes had just continued to use Wayne sparingly as a sub, introducing him at the end of games when teams were tiring and when the youngster's speed and strength could do the maximum damage. Wayne was becoming increasingly frustrated at the situation – he just wanted to start games and play as much as football as he could. Supremely confident, he always recognised that his unhappiness at not being involved in games was an important part of his football character. The limited period he was given did not really give him time to adjust to the tempo of the games. It could be said that the velocity of the game has increased since Wayne's first season, but even back then it was very fast and physical.

The young Everton striker thought that he had done enough in his previous appearances to warrant a starting place against the mighty Arsenal team. The bigger they come, the harder they fall, as his father used to say.

We hear a lot about Fake News these days, but back then there was no news on Wayne Rooney because Moyes forbade him from granting any interviews to the media or even appearing at the weekly press conferences. Wayne was not concerned about this because basically he was a very shy person and he did his 'talking' on the pitch. Moyes wanted to keep him under wraps for as long as he could.

What of Coleen? How was his budding relationship progressing? Strangely enough it had started to come together around the time he had made his debut against Spurs, when they started dating. Still in full-time education, the school holidays gave her more time to be with the shy lad from the neighbourhood.

A huge contingent of Rooneys had assembled for the Arsenal game, for it was the biggest match of the season for them so far. Arsenal were the double winners and were smashing records with contemptuous ease. In their previous away game they had thrashed Leeds 4–1 to eclipse Brian Clough's Nottingham Forest's record of twenty-two away games without loss. The Leeds manager Terry Venables was awestruck, saying that he had never seen anything 'as good as that'. Comparisons were being drawn to the great Ajax team of the seventies and the total football of Johan Cruyff. They emphasised the value of using great speed, football intelligence and razor-sharp passing skills to outwit their opponents.

Wayne entered the field to the familiar strains of the fictional TV police series *Z Cars* theme tune, which had been adopted as the club's anthem in the same way that Gerry and the Pacemakers' hit ballad 'You'll Never Walk Alone' was synonymous with the team down the road. *Z Cars* was a sixties TV police drama set in Liverpool. A sort of Scouse version of the American *Hill Street Blues*, one of its early stars was the famous actor Brian Blessed, who does those amusing Warburton adverts about toasties. The theme was recorded by the Johnny Keating Orchestra and nudged the Top 40. Tony Blackburn, the popular veteran DJ, plays it occasionally on his *Sounds of the 60s* Radio 2 programme.

Wayne had heard the song countless times when he had gone to the games as a young supporter, yet now, when he was actually part of it all, it sounded somehow different.

The teams that day were:

Everton
Richard Wright, David Unsworth, David Weir, Joseph Yobo, Tony Hibbert, Thomas Gravesen, Lee Carsley, (Stubbs 90), Li Tie, Mark Pembridge, Kevin Campbell, Tomasz Radzinski, (Rooney 80)
Arsenal
Seaman, Lauren, Campbell, Cygan, Cole, Ljungberg, (Edu 85), Silva ,Viera, Touré (Wiltord 64), Henry, Kanu, (Jeffers71)
The referee was one of the best of his time – Uriah Rennie.

Winger Freddie Ljunberg gave Arsenal an early lead after a mistake by Unsworth. Kanu, playing in place of the injured Dennis Bergkamp, was allowed space to setup the Swede for a simple goal. It was the forty-ninth consecutive match that Arsenal had scored in. Midfielder Lee Carsley hit the post and the ball rebounded out to Radzinski, who held off Ashley Cole to equalise with a confident finish.

OH, WHAT A PERFECT DAY

As the game wore on Rooney became more agitated. He was desperate to be involved in the action but the clock was ticking in several ways. It was five days until his birthday and Wayne was anxious to notch his first Premier League goal before he attained the age of seventeen. Arsenal had chances to have won the match and keep their unbeaten record intact. Thierry Henry missed an easy chance from close in and then Sylvain Wiltord hit a post. Wayne could only watch on in horror as Fran Jeffers replaced Kanu with twenty minutes left.

At the time of writing this book, Franny was back at Everton teaching in the Academy, observing another generation of Academy boys, rather like a prospector sifting the water at the bottom of the river looking for gold. Funny how both men's paths led back there. Jeffers's career was seen by many as a 'cautionary tale for what can happen to teen prodigies'. Franny Jeffers, a self-confessed 'bit of a wild child', had rotten luck with shoulder and ankle injuries, which were taking their toll even before his move down to London.

To put it in musical terms, if Wayne was Paul McCartney then Franny Jeffers was Tommy Quickly. Aspiring popstar Tommy came from the same stable as the Beatles. Managed by Brian Epstein, he was seen as the next big musical sensation. He had the looks and the talent plus the infrastructure behind him that had made the four mop-tops from Liverpool the biggest band in the world. Yet, for whatever reason, Tommy never made it.

Back to the margins again.

Eventually, with barely ten minutes left, Moyes sent

Rooney on for Tomasz Radzinski. Alan Stubbs, a fellow sub, wished him luck. Immediately the crowd was lifted by the entrance of the local lad, who proceeded to get busy with the Arsenal defence, challenging and harrying. The game appeared to be heading for stalemate when in the last minute Thomas Gravesen lobbed the ball forward. Whether or not he intended to find Wayne nobody was ever really sure, but it dropped conveniently for our hero about thirty yards from the Arsenal goal. The Arsenal defence, instead of closing him down, backed off, content for him to have possession at that distance, because long-range shooting had been discouraged in the modern game since the time when Bobby Charlton was in his heyday. The Arsenal back four of that era was formidable, something their modern-day counterparts could learn from. Their defenders moved swiftly and bravely to block even the hardest shots. Plus, they had one of the best goalkeepers in the business. The Arsenal defence was entitled to feel reasonably secure, thinking that Rooney would either elect to pass or, being a beginner, abdicate from the responsibility of shooting.

They were wrong.

He veered fractionally to the left. Then drove the ball almost angrily over Seaman's head against the underside of the bar and into the roof of the net.

David Seaman was now thirty-nine and his best days were behind him, and it was to be his last season playing for Arsenal and England. A few days earlier he had played in a Euro qualifier against Macedonia and let a goal in directly from a corner. The Everton crowd did not let him forget that one. Was he to blame for the goal? If you *YouTube* the moment, you can see him on the ground, twisting his neck to look up at the ball bouncing around in the back of the net. He had probably dealt with harder shots, but nothing hit so venomously. It's funny that goalkeepers are not remembered so much for the shots they saved, but more for the ones that beat them. Seaman, despite his brilliant career, will almost always be remembered most for being beaten by Nayim's lob from the halfway line in the European Cup Winners' Cup final, or else for Wayne's shot whistling past him.

Wayne always maintained that he had been aiming for the far corner. You see in a manner of speaking, Rooney scored goals 'that were not there'. Goals that defied logic, goals that served to underline the scale of his unfathomable genius. And the home crowd, stunned at first, were almost disbelieving at what they had just seen. Like Seaman, they were not really sure how the ball had ended up where it had. Wayne was running towards them now, like Liam Gallagher at Knebworth when he left the stage to meet his people, all 250,000 of them. Both wanted to be part of something they had created, an out-of-body experience.

Then the roar started.

It was as if King Kong had dropped out of the sky and ripped the roof off the Gwladys Road Stand. Wayne's mum Jeanette, who was high up in that stand, burst into tears, whilst his dad just stood there shaking his head, a head full of the greats of Everton Football Club. Some he had witnessed in action, for instance Joe Royle, whereas others he had heard the stories about. Alex Young heading the title winner against Tottenham, or the greatest Evertonian of them all, Dixie Dean, who had scored fifty goals a season on three separate occasions. Now his flesh and blood was part of that proud history of achievement.

Wenger used the post-match press conference to heap praise on Wayne Rooney, saying that, 'At that age Rooney is already a complete footballer. The guy can play. He is the best English player under twenty I have seen since I came here.'

Fast forward to October 2004 and Wayne was in the red of Manchester United when they took on Arsenal, who had put together the amazing run of forty-nine consecutive top-flight games without defeat. After seventy-three minutes he went down in the penalty area after a challenge by Sol Campbell. Referee Mike Riley awarded one of the most controversial penalties in the history of the Premier, which Ruud van Nistelrooy converted. Wayne wrapped it up in the last minute, scoring from a break away, and afterwards in the tunnel the infamous 'pizzagate' incident occurred, where Sir Alex was hit by a slice of Domino's finest. Years later, Cesc Fàbregas, one of Wayne's most admired opponents, put his hands up as being responsible for the incident. Wenger and Arsenal had good reason to rue the day Wayne Rooney first kicked a ball in anger.

Wayne's goal could hardly have been a more dramatic introduction to the big time. For a period, the talk was that here was a young player who could operate at the same rarefied levels as Dixie Dean. After the celebrations in the dressing room he had to push his way through the crowd that had gathered outside to wish him well. He had a quiet night in, sitting with his family and his girlfriend, with people kept coming to the door to congratulate him. *Match of the Day* kept re-running footage of the goal. No matter how many times it was shown, Seaman was no nearer saving it.

CHAPTER 11

RHINO DAYS

'I watched him waddling onto the coach. He's a glorified
PE teacher who shouldn't be in charge of a men's team.'
JOEY BARTON, ON DAVID UNSWORTH

So, David Unsworth was in charge for Everton's next
game: a trip to Stamford Bridge in the Carabao Cup
three days after Ronald Koeman had been sacked. Rooney,
in his slate grey kit, was so keen to get started against
the champions that he jumped the gun, running into the
Chelsea half before the game had begun. The kick-off was
retaken and Wayne spent the early part of the game chasing
everything that moved.

Chelsea went in front after twenty-five minutes with a soft
goal conceding from a short corner. Their Brazilian winger
William worked the ball to Charly Musonda, one of their
promising youngsters who'd been given a start that night.

The Belgium Under-21 sent over a perfect cross that Antonio Rüdiger, the German defender, fired home with his right foot. It was another costly error by Ashley Williams, who had allowed Rudiger to drift away from him at a crucial moment.

Unsworth was furious since he had demanded before the game that Everton played at a greater tempo than they had under Koeman. His manifesto for Everton was to make them more solid by utilising the pressing game. The problems he had to overcome were the sloppy mistakes at the back that had led to so many goals being conceded and the fact that they were lightweight up front.

Wayne played deep that night but the lack of pace and experience up front made it hard for him. It had been clear all season that they lacked any true spark up front, with Lukaku not having been replaced. The drab first half petered out, but Everton came out after the interval with a fighting spirit. Wayne almost equalised in Everton's first serious attack. Jonjoe Kenny crossed from the right, Mirallas, now restored to the team, cushioned a gentle header towards Wayne, who instantly volleyed at goal. Unfortunately, his shot was blocked by Willy Caballero, the ex-Man City goalkeeper. It was a fine save, since Wayne had hit it sweetly.

Rooney's presence was unsettling the defenders and substitute Cesc Fàbregas would almost have headed into his own goal but for another smart stop by Caballero. Lennon almost equalised for Everton when Mirallas's cross fell kindly for him and he smacked the ball forward but the Chelsea defender Kennedy blocked it. Unsworth shuffled the pack in an attempt to get back in the game and brought

Calvert-Lewin on for James McCarthy. Calvert-Lewin was wearing one of those mask things to protect his face after a recent injury. The youngster took his place at centre-forward alongside Wayne, who was in his traditional Number 10 role.

An inexplicable error by him almost gave Chelsea their second goal. Wayne played a poor back pass straight to the Chelsea striker Batshuayi, who raced through and went around Jordan Pickford. The Blues striker looked certain to score but Phil Jagielka, rolling back the years to when he one of the fastest defenders in the country, managed to get back and block the shot, thereby saving a certain goal and Rooney's reputation.

That was Wayne's last action in the game because Unsworth decided to flex his newly grown muscles and took him off after eighty-two minutes. He was replaced by the Senegalese striker Oumar Niasse, the former Koeman outcast. As Wayne trudged off the pitch he looked across to the technical area where Unsworth stood and gave him a long stare. Unsworth appeared to be making a point by subbing the most famous player in his squad. A player with an awesome collection of honours and who was, to use the overworked expression, a legend.

Unsworth had no respect for his predecessor Koeman's methods or some of the players he had brought to the club. The ex-defender wanted to give opportunities to the younger members of the squad, prospects who he had been instrumental in bringing through from the Academy. In the closing minutes Lookman, Baningime and Davies were on the pitch, whilst Koeman's expensive summer purchases, Keane and Sigurdsson, were unused substitutes, stewing on the bench.

Where did this leave Wayne Rooney? In no man's land. An expensive acquisition certainly, but also the most famous and successful graduate from the Academy. In the closing minutes both sides scored. Chelsea wrapped the game up in the dying seconds – another corner was their undoing. Fàbregas and William exchanged passes before the Brazilian curled a great shot past Pickford.

That appeared to be that. However there was still time for Everton to do what they should have done much earlier: attack. They pushed up through the middle and attacked the heart of the Chelsea defence. Niasse charged through in best rhino fashion and the ball fell for the masked man Calvert-Lewin to tuck home, making it 2–1.

Everton have never won this competition. This was the sixth time Chelsea had beaten them in it.

David Gerald Unsworth was bullish at the end of the match despite Everton exiting the Carabao Cup. He told the *Metro*: 'Nobody likes losing games. I am a bad loser but I have to say I am proud of the performance, they were terrific. We think we had chances to get something from the game.'

What of Wayne? Well, it was his birthday on Tuesday, 24 October, his thirty-second year on planet earth. There were no celebrations though, since Coleen was away and the Chelsea match was the next day. On the Wednesday he boarded the 305 train to London from Runcorn. After the match he travelled home and did not arrive back in

RHINO DAYS

Prestbury until the early hours of Thursday morning. It was a 'Home Alone' scenario, what with Coleen and the kids holidaying in Barbados. Normally he would have had a lie-in because Everton would have given him the day off to rest up in readiness for Sunday's tricky-looking away game to 2016 champions Leicester City. No such luck for Wayne though, as he had to repay his debt to society as regards the serving of one hundred hours of community service.

An early-morning call awoke him and a chauffeured top-of-the range Audi took him on a three-mile journey to a community garden centre for adults with learning difficulties. This was in Macclesfield, where he started his duties.

The press must have been tipped off because pictures were splashed across the tabloids the next day of him arriving at the centre. Wayne was wearing a tracksuit the claret colour of West Ham shirts and pristine white trainers. He walked quickly, head bowed, in through the entrance of the centre, where a fellow was shovelling mud into a large wheelbarrow. Fag in his mouth, wearing shorts and a navy work shirt, he could have been a staff member or one of the community servicers. Perhaps he was already expecting Wayne to appear that morning but in any event, he recognised one of the most famous faces this side of the Mersey. He mumbled something to Wayne, probably a few words about football. Perhaps he was an Everton fan or, less likely, a Chelsea fan. Wayne blanked him. Well, it was early, and less than twelve hours ago he had been down in London playing against the champions of England, a team funded by one of the world's richest private citizens.

What exactly did he do there? Was there some *Cool Hand Luke* deal, where he was working on a chain gang, breaking rocks in the hot sun? It was nothing so dramatic. He was painting benches. What colour? Royal Blue? Surely not red? The truth was that Wayne was rubbish at DIY; he admitted that himself in his autobiography. Coleen had told the *Daily Star* at the start of the season that, 'I cannot rely on him to do anything. He doesn't help with the housework. Wayne does not put the rubbish out. He forgets to do things I ask him. I'll say "Will you post a letter on the way to training?" A week later the letter will still be in his car.'

In his interview with Alan Brazil on talkSPORT he gave some insight into the community service, saying, 'I enjoy doing it. Helping adults with learning difficulties. Working with people. I will keep in touch when I have done my hours. The staff are doing a fantastic job, made me feel so welcome. Did not even talk about football in there.'

It must have been relaxing for him, not to be Wayne Rooney for a while. Not to answer the same old questions about this goal or that match. You're a fan, you bought this book. If you were in Wayne's company, what would you talk to him about? Ninety per cent for sure it would be about football. Maybe you saw his goal against Arsenal or watched him in the white shirt with three lions on it and would want to discuss it with him. I wonder how many people asked him about the bicycle kick against Manchester City. Wayne made an impact wherever he went and people talked to him about it.

So it must have been nice for somebody to talk to him

about his favourite soap *EastEnders* or the merits of the latest Stereophonics recording. I had a chum who used to drink with another Manchester United legend – perhaps the biggest: George Best. My friend knew nothing about football, but he knew who George was because he was the first celebrity footballer, some even called him the fifth Beatle. He was the first footballer to make the transition from the newspaper's back page to the front. George was retired by then, living in London with one of his Miss Worlds. My friend and George would meet in a quiet pub off Jermyn Street and just discuss world events or swap drinking stories. Not once was football ever mentioned.

Wayne returned to the garden centre again the next day for another six-hour stint. This time he was wearing a blue jacket with matching bottoms and a pair of black trainers, possibly Puma. No JPG suits or handmade shoes. The Everton superstar arrived at 8.40 a.m. and left at 3.04 p.m. I'm not sure whether or not he had a meal break. The staff at the centre must have been used to having famous footballers there because Carlos Tevez, his former Manchester United strike partner, served time there. The Argie ace was given a community service order in 2013 after he was caught driving whilst serving a ban. I don't know if they put a 'Welcome to Macclesfield' poster up for him. Carlos was currently in China plying his trade for one of the footballers' 'retirement home' teams that had tried to lure Rooney.

A selection of bosses continued to be linked with the job of manager. Burnley's gruff-voiced supremo Sean Dyche was the frontrunner. The joke going the rounds was that if he were to land the job then the Toffees would be renamed the Strepsils. Unsworth was still in the frame because of his close association with chairman Bill Kenwright and the owner, Farhad Moshiri. Formerly the business partner of Usmanov, he had previously shared the Arsenal investment but sold his shares to him in 2016 and now owned 49.6 per cent of Everton.

David Moyes had flourished at Everton because of his close relationship with Kenwright, the ex-actor who'd been in the TV soap opera *Coronation Street*. In his early days at the club he once visited Kenwright's home to discuss their mutual vision of Everton. Legend has it that they stayed up most of the night chatting, fuelled by the chairman's cheese on toast. The complete support of Kenwright had enabled Moyes to stay afloat at Everton through even the rockiest of times.

Unsworth wanted to return his new charges back to the 'Dogs of War' style that Wayne had watched from the terraces. He even had the T-shirt. In an interview with *The Sun* the forty-four-year-old caretaker boss explained his mindset based on a heavy work ethic, saying, 'I like a smile around the place, an atmosphere where players feel free to express themselves. But at the same time, within a structure where the minimum requirement is 100 per cent effort.'

Leicester easily beat Everton 2–0 at the King Power Stadium; they also had their own managerial musical chairs game going. Another ex-Southampton manager, the Frenchman Claude Puel, had taken the reins on the same day that Everton had been dumped out of the Carabao Cup,

Craig Shakespeare having been sacked a few days before. Shakespeare, who had replaced the title winning Claudio Ranieri, was to end up at Everton in the coming months as the managerial carousel gathered speed. Puel, so often portrayed as a dour, solemn figure, was all smiles as his team outplayed a shambolic Everton.

The team went ahead after just eighteen minutes, thanks to some slick work by their dynamic duo of Riyad Mahrez and Jamie Vardy. Leighton Baines took a free kick, hoping that Wayne could have got on the end of it, but the ball was cleared to the Leicester 'flying machine' Demarai Gray. The winger motored sixty yards through the Everton rearguard without a serious challenge being put against him to feed the Leicester playmaker Riyad Mahrez. (This was a few weeks before he had adopted that strange 'Debbie Harry' blond hairstyle.) Mahrez spun away from the Everton midfielder Idrissa Gueye, who Unsworth had been trying to secure on a new long-term deal, and sent over a perfect cross to James Vardy. The England striker, one of the replacement options for Wayne, buried the chance instantly. The goal led to a heated debate amongst the Everton defenders, plus a lot of furious gesticulating and finger pointing.

Ten minutes later the game was over. In that time, Gray hit a cross after walking past Davies. Jonjoe Kenny mistimed his attempted clearance and sliced the ball horribly. The parabola took the ball over Pickford and it dropped into the back of the net. Kenny was grief-stricken, rubbing his hands into his short hair, for he was seen as one of Everton's brightest prospects. The young defender's form had been one of the few constant factors in a troubled season.

Everton stormed downfield and should have been back in the game within minutes but for a bad mistake by the referee Andre Marriner. Leicester's wing-back, Christian Fuchs, brought down Aaron Lennon in the box, but no penalty was awarded. Rooney was furious at the decision: only a few yards from the incident, he turned and threw his arms wide, like an opera singer soliciting adoration. He started to berate the officials for their failure to spot a blatant penalty.

In that season hardly a week went by without some controversy about a disputed decision. Arsène Wenger had a running battle with the FA throughout the season about what he considered to be refereeing errors that had cost Arsenal vital points. The problem was that now, with the increasing velocity of the game, the middle-aged referees just could not keep up with the play.

Aaron Lennon was one of the quickest players in the Premier. It was good to see him back in the team after his problems, and he was one of eight Englishmen fielded by Unsworth that day. Everton improved in the second half, having more possession, but unfortunately did not trouble the Leicester keeper, Kasper Schmeichel. Wayne was again substituted by Unsworth and again looked unhappy at the prospect. The camera focused on him later, sitting in the dugout wearing his Everton parka, hands rubbing his brow and glaring, as if to say: 'Gimme a break'.

The Everton Rubik-cube puzzle of Wayne/Sigurdsson/ Klaassen was focused on again in the post-match analysis.

Most fans agreed with Unsworth's assertion that the trio could not play in the same side. It was a problem that Koeman could not solve in his spell in charge and one of the main reasons why he lost his job. Rather than squeeze them all into his team, Unsworth insisted that he would play his men in their proper positions. Thus, Wayne started against Leicester with Sigurdsson on the bench and poor Davy Klaassen not even in the squad. It was all a tad surreal, with the club's biggest star and two hugely expensive signings who were unable to gel.

Joey Barton was very critical of Unsworth. Joey is a true Evertonian, who was portrayed in the media as a product of a cityscape of council houses, rough pubs, tough kids. The scars of his failure to make it through the Everton Academy remained with him all his life. In his excellent biography, *No Nonsense*, he launched a scathing attack on Neil Dewsnip, who ran the Everton Academy, saying that, 'He represented everything I resented.'

Perhaps he saw Unsworth as being part of that football hierarchy.

Wayne's performance against Leicester drew criticism on social media. He was all over the pitch as he kept dropping back in a vain attempt to spark something. The jury was still out on how effective he could be as an orthodox striker at that level. Fifteen years at the sharp end and his body was nearly in bits, but his mind was still razor-sharp. His age was counting against him to be the focal striker and Unsworth's dispassionate eyes saw him more in a supporting role. The fact was now though that he was spending increasing time in deep midfield in some de-facto holding and Everton needed him to be scoring.

CHAPTER 12

NORTHERN SOUL

'Who wants the truth? That's what show biz is for – to prove that's it's not what you are that counts. It's what you think you are.'

ANDY WARHOL

NOVEMBER 2002

In an interview with the *Daily Mail* shortly after Wayne Rooney had returned to Everton, David Moyes was asked about his most vivid memory of him. Without hesitation Moyes spoke of a late goal his striker had scored for Everton against Leeds in November 2002, saying: 'It was the only goal of the game, at a place where we never seemed to win.' Moyes was silent for a moment, reflecting on a special moment in his relationship with Wayne, his extraordinary periwinkle-blue eyes sparkling. 'There is this great picture of him celebrating with the supporters. It's the only picture I asked Wayne to sign. I have always kept it.'

Somewhere in the Moyes' archives in his beautiful home, there is a picture of Wayne, arms outstretched, being mobbed by Evertonians. In the captured image he has just scored a goal as important to them as the one that smashed Arsenal's unbeaten record. Even though Leeds United have been marooned in the Championship for years, trapped in a Sargasso Sea of debt and mediocrity, certain fans of a certain age still regard the club as a prize scalp. To them, Leeds were the anti-Christ, or, to paraphrase Cruyff on José Mourinho, they were 'The enemies of football'.

The fierce rivalry between the two clubs can be traced back to another November afternoon in 1964 when Everton had a home match versus the bellicose Leeds United, who were managed by Don Revie. The match went down in folklore as the 'Battle of Goodison'. Everton's Sandy Brown was sent off and winger Derek Temple was hurt by a chest-high tackle by the Leeds defender, Bell. The furious Everton fans carpeted the pitch with bottles and the game was delayed when the referee took the teams off to cool down.

The two teams that played at Elland Road that Sunday afternoon when Wayne scored were as follows:

LEEDS
Robinson, Mills, Woodgate, Radebe, Lucic (Harte 45), Bowyer, Bakke, Barmby, Kewell, Viduka (Bridges 68), Smith
Manager: Terry Venables

EVERTON
Wright, Hibbert, Stubbs, Yobo, Unsworth, Carsley,
Linderoth, Tie Li (Naysmith 82), Pembridge,
Campbell, Radzinski (Rooney 75)

Wayne scored the winning goal eight minutes from time,
shortly after entering the game. Picking the ball up near the
halfway line, he surged past Leeds hardman Lee Bowyer and
set off for goal. He ran into the box and instantly dispatched
a low right-foot shot through the legs of the statuesque Lucas
Radebe and past the keeper, Paul Robinson. Delighted to
see it end up in the net, he celebrated with the huge army of
Everton fans clustered behind the goal. Fans even wanted to
pinch him to see if he was real. It just seemed unbelievable
that suddenly this young player had emerged to score
these amazing goals that could beat their bitterest foes.
The Rooney clan had travelled enmasse to Elland Road
and Wayne claimed he saw his Uncle Eugene celebrating
wildly in the midst of all the chaos. It was Everton's first
win at Elland Road in fifty-one years and Leeds's sixth game
without a win.

The Golden Bough: A Study in Comparative Religion
was a classic nineteenth-century study of mythology and
religion. In it, the anthropologist Sir James George Frazer
wrote that primitive civilisations associated themselves with
'magical man-gods' who could provide food and water.
To put this concept in more simplistic terms: if you want
success, associate yourself with someone successful. Rooney
was now a symbol, a metaphor for success against the odds.

In a dull first half Everton just edged it, and Leeds midfielder Nick Barmby received a yellow card for diving. Barmby was an ex-Everton player who had left to go to Liverpool and received plenty of abuse that day from the travelling bluenoses. The Everton manager at the time, Walter Smith, recognised that Barmby was not from the City and failed to understand the passion involved. This was surprising, since in Glasgow he had managed the waspish Rangers, and Rangers and Celtic rivalry was always a major factor in inter-club dealings.

Harry Kewell was a constant threat but the Everton keeper was on good form. Radzinski had a couple of chances that he should have scored from and he was substituted to make way for Rooney. The Pole had been highly impressed with the embryonic Wayne when he started training with the first team. Tomasz thought at first that Rooney had been overwhelmed by being in the Premier League at such a young age. He is quoted in *Faith of our Families: Everton FC, an Oral history* by James Corbett (De Coubertin Books) as saying, 'But whatever he was showing us in training, he was still twice as impressive as when he was playing actually in his first minutes in the Premier League, this is how good he was.'

Sandwiched between Wayne's winners against Arsenal and Leeds, the Toffees had another good victory away to West Ham at Upton Park. Wayne, despite his sensational performance in the previous game, was left on the bench. Shrewdly, Moyes was still determined to keep the spotlight off him and let him progress at his own rate, because he was fully aware of the dips in form and the sudden loss of confidence that could affect youngsters.

The West Ham team included some really class players who would walk into their current squad: Michael Carrick, Jermaine Defoe, Paulo Di Canio and Joe Cole. The latter could stand comparison with Rooney, in that he was probably the missing link between him and Gazza. Seen as the next big thing, Joe was a timelessly fascinating player, arguably the best of his generation. But sadly, despite his eventual transfer to Chelsea and a stack of honours, he never fulfilled his vast early potential.

It was a dull game played in blustery conditions with very little goalmouth action. The first real chance of the match fell on the hour to the Italian ace Paolo di Canio, who hit the ball straight at the Everton goalkeeper Richard Wright. That was the signal for Moyes to wave on Wayne to substitute for guess who? You've got it – Radzinski. Almost immediately he nearly scored, racing on a neat flick by Campbell to fire inches over the bar. What a start! At that time he was a force of nature, unstoppable, just sheer power. The whole team seemed lifted by his electric presence and perplexed by his lack of game time.

Within six minutes of his introduction Everton had scored. The man called 'Rhino' crossed to the far post and the Republic of Ireland star Lee Carsley rose to thump home a header. Wayne was one of the first players to congratulate him, as Lee had done the same thing when Rooney opened his Everton account at Wrexham.

Near the end, the enigmatic Joe Cole, who had played

a subdued match, suddenly exploded into action. He burst into the Everton penalty area and fired in a fierce shot that goalkeeper Wright made a great save from. As the players left the field, Joe nodded across to Wayne, mouthing, 'Well played.' Wayne smiled back – well, he gave his idea of a smile. The two young gunslingers were checking each other out, and both were to figure prominently for their country in the future – in fact they were pivotal members of the 'Golden Generation'.

Three days after their win at Elland Road, Everton knocked Newcastle out of the Worthington Cup 3–2 on penalties. That was after the match had finished 3–3 after extra time. Wayne was excited to have started the game with Radzinski relegated to the subs bench. He contributed to the first goal by forcing a corner which Kevin Campbell nodded home after escaping the attention of his marker. That appeared to be enough to settle the tie until a late two-goal flurry by Newcastle's Kieron Dyer turned the game on its head.

They had reckoned without Wayne's persistence though. And with just five minutes left to play, he surged impressively forward and found some space on the right, instantly crossing for Steve Watson, himself an ex-Newcastle player, to side-foot home. The game went into extra time and on the one-hundred-minute mark a tangle in the Everton defence led to Alessandro Pistone conceding an own goal. Defeat remained mockingly near but the good thing was that Everton had a Rhino on the pitch. In the second half of extra time Wayne bludgeoned home a penalty to take the game to penalties, if that makes sense.

In the penalty shoot-out Unsworth took the first of the spot-kicks, which was maybe not such a good idea, as he blasted yards wide. Everton dug in though, and Wayne chipped in with a coolly taken effort. Watson and the redoubtable Kevin Campbell scored from their attempts. Richard Wright became the hero of the hour, saving kicks from Hugo Viana and Laurent Robert. In the end it finished 3–2 to the Toffees and the reward for their rabbit-from-hat performance was a trip to Chelsea in the next round.

The evening was also a triumph for Wayne. He had assisted in setting up two goals in normal time and contributed with a penalty. Perhaps even more importantly, he had played for two hours, which proved his bulldog resilience and durability. Six years later, he scored in the penalty shoot-out when Manchester United beat Chelsea in the first all-British Champions League final. I wonder which was the most pressured situation for him?

Everton's winning streak continued with two solitary goal victories over Charlton at home and Blackburn away. They made it six wins in a row when they beat West Bromwich at Goodison in the last week of November. That was the first time that Wayne ever received any adverse criticism in the press. The Toffees were leading 1–0, courtesy of a Radzinski goal. Wayne came on for his usual late cameo. Within seconds he was running down the line, hotly pursued by West Brom's Darren Moore. Wayne saw this as a good chance to demonstrate his ball skills and entertain the chilled Everton faithful. Checking his stride, he proceeded to taunt Moore by putting his foot on the ball, hands on his hips, and inviting him to take it off him. I have seen Charlie Cooke of Chelsea do this to Billy Bremner and Bobby Moore in high-pressure situations. Is it cockiness or supreme confidence, I wonder.

Wayne then burst past the West Bromwich man and fizzed in a shot. The next day Moore was all over the press, criticising Rooney for disrespecting him.

Such behaviour was ascribed to being due to the arrogance of youth. However, in his defence Wayne was merely playing as he had always played the game. Since his emergence he had captured the imagination of the football world by performing in exactly the same fashion as he had when he was first in the Academy. That is why he was such a refreshing change. He was just barnstorming, attacking, dribbling through packed defences, and smashing in shots from all angles. If you go back still further, that is how he played in the Liverpool streets. Jimmy Martin had always insisted that he was the 'last of the street footballers'.

Martin recalled that after Wayne had finished training with the Academy he would drop him off home. Before he went in for his supper though, he would run off and play with his mates in the street. Rooney had been shaped by the traditions and lore of the City of Liverpool and also those of Everton Football Club.

In one of those fixture quirks Everton returned to the scene of their recent Worthington Cup victory: St James Park, for a Premier League fixture against the 'Black and Whites'. They were looking for their seventh straight win that would have pushed them into second place above

Liverpool. Wayne was again named as a substitute because Moyes was still using him as an impact player and nursing him along.

Kevin Campbell gave Everton the start they wanted, putting Everton in front just as he had three weeks before. In fact, he had scored against Newcastle in his last five visits there. The hopes of three points receded though when Yobo was sent off after pulling down Craig Bellamy, the live-wire Newcastle striker. Wayne was watching Bellamy closely from his vantage point on the bench, and realised that they shared a few traits. Both were highly skilled but also had an fiery manner and the goal-hunting instincts of a predator.

Bellamy at that point was the perfect foil for Alan Shearer, and together they were a lethal combination, the former's pace and strength dovetailing perfectly with the guile and experience of Shearer. Craig's fearsome, and sometimes monstrous mien, led to a falling-out with Shearer and his departure from Tyneside. Craig Bellamy is the only player to have scored for seven Premier League clubs. Everton were one of the five Premier sides that Mark Hughes scored his goals for.

Alan Shearer finished as the highest ever goal scorer in the Premier League, and he was the only player to score more than thirty top-division goals in three successive seasons. Along with Andy Cole he shares the record for the most Premier League goals in a season: thirty-four. However, to put this in perspective, Dixie Dean scored sixty League goals for Everton in the lost world of 1927–28. And Jimmy

Greaves scored 420 goals for Chelsea, AC Milan, Tottenham and West Ham, 366 of them in the League.

When Wayne had scored his 200th Premier goal against Manchester City in his second game back for Everton it opened up the possibility of him becoming Shearer's only peer at the summit of goal scorers. Shearer equalised for Newcastle against Everton just when it looked like they would hold on for victory. Wright could do nothing to stop the goal driven in for twenty-two yards, six minutes from time.

Wayne had come on in the usual ploy of replacing Radzinski after seventy-three minutes. With only ten men, Everton struggled to work the ball forward. They had no heat maps at that time, but if they had, they would have demonstrated Rooney's average position in the last quarter of the game, which would have been in the Everton half. Occasionally he would scamper forward to the final third. Moyes to some extent considered Wayne as an attacking midfielder because he could play incisive passes and had great dribbling qualities. Wayne always preferred to play on the shoulder of the last defender, stretching their back four, attacking all the time.

It was Bellamy who won it for Newcastle though. With just two minutes left, he fired in a shot that deflected off Li Tie and went past a stranded Richard Wright. At the final whistle Wayne was upset – he always was when he finished on the losing side, his fierce pride getting jumbled up with his emotional frailty. Shearer looked across at him as they trudged off the field like exhausted GIs returning from the battlefield. Neither had any indication that Wayne would emerge as his token replacement in the England team as the main striker, and would also hunt down his fabulous goal-scoring record.

One Newcastle player made a special point of going over to console the youngster: another legend, Gary Speed. The Welshman only had a couple of years at Goodison but left an indelible mark after being signed by Joe Royle just before the 1996–97 season. Like Wayne, he had been an Everton fan since he could walk – a tradition carried on by one of his sons. Gary made an instant impact, finishing joint top scorer with Duncan Ferguson and was voted Player of the Year. The following season, Howard Kendall succeeded Joe as manager and appointed Gary as club captain, and he looked set to rule the roost for years. His reign was short-lived though, and the following January he was sold to Newcastle, then managed by Kenny Dalglish.

More conspiracy theories abounded about the reason for his abrupt departure than those surrounding the assassination of President John F Kennedy. The consensus was that following an altercation with Howard Kendall, he refused to travel to West Ham for a game and then left the club. Both men have now passed away, and the secret died with them, but in the book *Faith of Our Families: Everton FC, an Oral History* (see above), Kendall's words on the subject were:

There was no real bust up. It was a messy transfer, complicated by the fact that he was the club captain and a lifelong Everton supporter. I did not want to lose him, he was one of my best players. It was not clear whether I would ever see the money his sale generated.

Wayne was still working his way through the ranks when this was happening but Speed was a familiar and popular figure at the Academy, encouraging and advising people. He was always supportive and interested in nurturing the talents of the youngsters. Speed believed in the instilling of a sense of discipline and a highly competitive edge. In a world often fuelled by self-aggrandisement, the Welshman was an absolute gentleman. Often, he would nod over to Wayne senior and his son when he saw them at Bellefield, for even then the word was spreading about how special this young prodigy was.

The last time Gary Speed saw Wayne Rooney was on 26 November 2011. Wayne was in a red shirt playing against Speed's old club, Newcastle United, at Old Trafford. Alan Shearer sat with him and they watched as Wayne set up the first goal with a fierce drive. It ricocheted off the keeper, Taylor, allowing Javier Hernández to score. Demba Ba equalised for Newcastle from the penalty spot. After the match Gary drove home to Huntington, Cheshire.

The next morning his wife Louise found him dead in his garage. He had hanged himself.

A consummate professional (only Ryan Giggs had played in more Premier League games), Gary Andrew Speed had trained himself during all of his short life to show no sign of real emotion. Perhaps he had decided to kill himself for a long time, but he had concealed his intentions so well, so carefully. The Evertonian's tragic death hit so many people hard because they felt that the noblest virtues he epitomised, camaraderie and dependability, were being eroded in the shark tank of what is now modern football, a cesspool of greed and duplicity.

CHAPTER 13

BETTER CALL SAM

'His favourite book is Wayne Rooney's
autobiography.' 'He's a good writer, Wayne.'
COLDFEET, SERIES 7

Wayne Rooney and Everton were always good for a
name-check in popular culture. Actor James Nesbitt,
in real life a huge Manchester United fan, slotted that line
into the latest series of Mike Bullen's comedy drama series,
Cold Feet. Even the character Phelan, the Scouse serial
killer in the TV soap opera *Coronation Street*, peppered his
dialogue with a reference to being as 'nervous as a Liverpool
fan in Gwladys Street'.

As the late autumn turned to early winter it looked like
it was going to be a hard one for Everton. The latest joke
was that David Unsworth insisted that his players were
the fittest in the Premier League because he made them do

training laps around him. Poor old Dave, he could already feel the crosshairs on his forehead.

The interim manager admitted that he was completely in the dark about who would be the permanent successor to the sacked Ronald Koeman. The press carried reports that Everton were already talking to the ex-England boss Sam Allardyce. Unsworth told the *Metro*: 'We just carry on day by day, game by game. What we want is the best resolution for Everton. It's a fabulous job at a fabulous club.'

Everton suffered their own Brexit when Lyon easily beat them 3–0 to send the Merseysiders crashing out of the Europa League with two games left. Wayne was left out of the debacle and did not even travel to France. Other senior members of the squad not included for the game were Leighton Baines, Michael Keane and Phil Jagielka. Unsworth explained that they had played a lot of games and he wanted to freshen it up by giving a chance to players who had been agitating for one.

His main ploy was to play Gylfi Sigurdsson as a 'false nine'. The club's record signing tried hard in a role that was possibly earmarked for Rooney, but his chances were limited and he was given little opportunity to shine.

In a tepid first half, Everton did well to contain the technically capable Lyon and it was all square at the break. However, the roof fell in midway through the second half, when their dangerman Bertrand Traoré scored. Enter Memphis Depay, their tormentor-in-chief at Goodison. He made the second goal for Aouar and near the end headed a third. To complete the gloom, Morgan Schneiderlin, having a poor season, was sent off. Unsworth turned on his players, accusing them of 'caving in'. In four games they had managed to accumulate only one point and had conceded ten goals.

Wayne was back for the next Premier game at home to Watford on the following Sunday. How much he figured in Unsworth's plans was unclear. Joey Barton was still sniping at Unsworth: 'Everton were sloppy, like their interim manager.'

Only Wayne emerged unscathed from his criticism. Joey insisted that Rooney should never had been subbed at Leicester, and that up until then he had been their best player. Wayne did not give too much away to a Sky reporter, who asked him sardonically how he was feeling, when he was just shrugging his shoulders and cutting a solitary figure. How much fire he had in his belly was one of the questions being asked of him. To some he was a spent force, whilst others accentuated the positives of his return as a potential messiah.

Even more questions were being raised after sixty-four minutes, when Everton were 0–2 down to a classy-looking Watford side. A lacklustre Wayne was struggling to make any impact in the game. As Everton fan Mike Burke said: 'At this stage I was expecting more of him.'

All the action and goals came in the second half after a tedious first forty-five minutes. The excellent left-winger Richarlison had put Watford ahead early in the second half with a fine strike. This man had been born in the notorious Vila Rubia in Nova Veneza, Brazil, and his parents had split up when he was very young. The future Premier star became the major breadwinner in his family and had resisted peer pressure to become involved in the heavy drug scene and murderous landscape where he lived. To escape that violent, treacherous environment and steer himself to the glitz of the Premier via a £11-million transfer from Fluminense was some journey. In contrast, Wayne came from a stable family background. However, the temptations for both men were the same because of the relentless forces of the drug culture.

Just before the hour the Watford goalkeeper, Gomes, sustained a head injury and left the field to be replaced by the Greek International keeper Orestis Karnezis. Christian Kabasele headed the second goal for Watford after sixty-four minutes following appalling marking. The home crowd turned on the team as they began unravelling. Unsworth took their superhero Rooney off, replacing him with Calvert-Lewin. Wayne looked unhappy at the decision and the crowd were subdued, many wondering why he should be squandering his talent on this dreck. Perhaps he was shell-shocked by the poor performance of their team, the whole debacle being almost too much to bear.

Within a few minutes a dreadful error by the substitute goalkeeper, who was making his debut in the Premier, put Everton back in the game. Another Everton sub, Ademola Lookman, hit over a hopeful lob. Karnezis raced out of his goal, missed the ball completely and Niasse walked the ball into the net. Six minutes later, Baines hit over a corner, which Karnezis failed to collect, and Dominic Calvert-Lewin headed a simple equaliser. In the ninety-first minute, fellow Greek defender José Holebas impeded Aaron Lennon with a toe-curling challenge and the referee awarded a penalty. If Wayne had still been on the field he would have taken it, but Leighton Baines was given his old job back and he powered home the winner.

The melodrama and the penalties continued though because the long delay caused by keeper Gomes's injury was added on and in the hundredth minute of the game Watford were awarded a penalty. Tom Cleverly, the ex-Toffees midfielder, elected to take the spot-kick. Signed from Manchester United on a five-year deal in 2015, injuries had limited his appearances in his first season on Merseyside. When Ronald Koeman took charge of the team Cleverley was not included in his plans, and the club had failed utterly to capitalise on his talents.

But the ex-England International fluffed his chance by blasting the ball wide. So Everton won a roller-coaster game and jumped up the table from nineteenth to fifteenth. Everton had pulled off a remarkable win, and the match stats indicated that in the second half Watford had almost twice the possession – 66 per cent, and total passes in the match of 470 compared to Everton's 290.

Rhino was absolutely delighted at the result and was almost hyperventilating from stress when he told *The Sun*: 'I have been the proudest man in the world to take charge and whatever happens now, no one can take that away from me. What will be will be.'

Or in the Spanish translation of the words, made famous

by the Doris Day song, 'Que Sera, Sera'. Everton were very keen on employing the Watford coach Marco Silva but were rebuffed. Farhad Moshiri was particularly anxious to install the Portuguese boss and had offered more than £10 million in compensation. Silva, who exuded brooding charisma, started in England with a short stint at relegated Hull. There was no release clause in his two-year contract with Watford. The Hornets were to go on to a terrible run with only one win in eleven games. It ended up with Silva being sacked in mid-January and Watford blamed Everton for the approach to Marco.

A statement by the club read: 'The catalyst for this decision is that unwarranted approach, something which the board believes has seen a significant deterioration in both focus and results.'

Speaking on *Match of the Day 2* after the news of Silva's sacking had broken, former Chelsea and England wing-back Graeme Le Saux commented that, 'It's unusual for one boardroom to criticise another.'

More available names were mentioned, including Louis van Gaal and Ralf Rangnick. With impeccable timing, Sam Allardyce had ruled himself out of the job, as he had tired of Everton's procrastination.

The following Saturday, Everton travelled to Selhurst Park to play Crystal Palace in a desperate relegation battle. The Eagles were now managed by Wayne's ex-England boss Roy Hodgson. Recalling his chronic tiredness, it had seemed unlikely that Hodgson would ever work again in the top flight after the disaster of his job as England manager. In their hour of need though, Palace turned to the seventy-year-old and it was in fact to be an inspired choice. For Hodgson, living quietly in his gated Surrey mansion, it seemed a strange decision to return to the heat of battle in the world's richest league, but Roy was a true football man. Frank de Boer was sacked after losing his first four games as another example of a Premier team being stung by a failed gamble on a Dutch manager. Crystal Palace had made the worst ever start in Premier League history, with the insidious menace of relegation already staring them in the face.

Wayne Rooney was dropped by Unsworth down to the substitutes bench with Niasse and Lookman starting up front. Everton fell behind in the first minute, as the Palace midfielder, Ruben Loftus-Cheek, on loan from Chelsea, powered through its galumphing back four and his shot was parried by Pickford. James McArthur easily scored from the rebound. Oumar Niasse had something to prove: he had been humiliated by Koeman, who had not even given him a personal locker. Palace had rejected him on transfer deadline day. He was starting his career all over again, and within a few minutes won another penalty when he was allegedly impeded by Scott Dann. For the second successive game Leighton Baines, sporting his mod-style sideburns, scored from the spot.

Baines, the ex-Wigan Athletic man, was still deadly from the spot but looking far from fit – defensively, his standards had fallen. The Palace wing-back, Joel Ward, was given far too much space by him and he exploited the situation by setting up Wilfried Zaha for the second Palace goal. Zaha took the goal neatly: his languid style of play had improved after Hodgson had switched him from the wing to centre-forward. For too long he had been squandering his talents.

Niasse was not giving up though and was determined to grasp his opportunity. In the dying seconds of the first half he equalised after an assist by Idrissa Gueye. That is how the game stayed, a point not really helping either side, such were their parlous states.

Rooney, restlessly watching the game from the bench, did not get onto the field. With fifteen minutes left Sandro went on for Lennon, when normally Rooney would have been expected to have been introduced. The press were quick to latch on to the wisdom, or the lack of it, displayed by Unsworth in his use of substitutes. The fans, however, were divided. Unsworth was making a statement by playing the youngsters, rather than the big-money signings. Where did this leave Wayne in the equation? Rumours were rife that there was a rift between the two men. Perhaps it went back to Wayne's early days at Everton, when he had nutmegged Rhino in the training session.

Yet Unsworth was quick to praise Rooney's 'fantastic' attitude. Wayne kept his own counsel, not wishing to rock the boat, instead taking to social media to share a picture of his son's eighth birthday celebrations.

Wayne was restored to the Everton game for the 'dead rubber' home game (meaning this one result wouldn't affect the eventual outcome) against Atalanta in the Europa League. It was one of nine changes from the Palace garden party.

On a cold mucky Mersey night that was pouring with rain, just 17,431 turned out, the second smallest European crowd ever at Goodison Park. The season was limping along, what might be described as a sort of 'Carry on Unsworth' period. Everton started brightly but the Italians, looking for their first away win in Europe in thirty years, went ahead after twelve minutes through their midfielder, Bryan Cristante. This was after a poor clearance from Ashley Williams enabled him to slice through. That was how it stayed at the break, and it was the sixteenth time in the last eighteen matches that Everton had conceded the first goal.

Michael Gray, the ex-Sunderland defender, was summarising for talkSPORT, who covered the match. Gray was of the opinion that Rooney had tried hard to make things happen but had to drop deeper to provide a fulcrum for other attackers to work around. The Everton keeper, Joel Robles, saved a penalty early in the second half after a reckless challenge by Williams on that man Cristante. There was no stopping him though, as he seemed to have the run of the home defence, and shortly afterwards he scored again. Sandro broke his duck to score his first goal for Everton and briefly revive hopes of a face-saving comeback. The Koeman management team thought that Sandro Ramírez, who had been bought from Malaga, would have been the solution to the loss of Romelu Lukaku.

Everton's House of Cards collapsed in the last five minutes though, as there came a late burst that took the hosts by surprise. The Atalanta sub, Robin Gosens, scored a glorious third with a dipping volley that gave Robles no chance. The

Toffees' agony was compounded by two late goals from the Danish striker Cornelius. The Serie A side had twenty shots in the match and in the end, it just turned out to be shooting practice for them.

It was the heaviest defeat in the UEFA/Europa League by an English side since the powerful German war machine of Bayern Munich had beaten Nottingham Forest by the same score in March 1996, with Klinsmann, a magnificent striker back in the day, scoring twice. Blackburn's ill-starred foray into the Champions League during the same season was the only time an English club had picked up such a low total of points in their first five games.

The fans were thumbing through their record books to find worse stats in the 'awfulness stakes'. It was the eighth straight game in all competitions that they had conceded two or more goals in a match. In their whole history, dating back to 1878, it was only the twenty-fifth time they had conceded five or more goals in a home match.

Unsworth now faced the wrath of the press and a barrage of abuse on social media. The talk was of a 'parochial minnow' and a porous Everton drowning and humiliated. There were suggestions that players were out of position, and the team was compared to a giant bowl of jelly that Unsworth could not stop wobbling. Wayne had a lot of credit with the fans, being arguably the best-loved and greatest Everton player of recent times. But the knives were being sharpened as the situation became toxic. In a short period, their form had gone from disappointing, to dismal, to desperate. Most matches in their current form looked unwinnable.

The club's search for a new boss was being further complicated by questions being asked regarding the legal technicalities of Farhad Moshiri's ownership and shareholding. Unsworth had now supervised four lamentable losses in the six games he was caretaking for and must have known that his time in that role was coming to an end. He had used the word 'fragile' about some of his players after the Atalanta game.

Talking to *The Independent*, Unsworth lamented the changes in the games since he had made the last of his over 300 appearances for Everton. He said: 'The game has changed since I played; there was a different mentality in the changing room then. I do not think as a manager you can shout and bawl all the time when a team is low on confidence – you have to be more selective in your approach.'

Could it get any worse? I am afraid it could. Everton travelled to St Mary's to play Southampton, who inflicted further misery by hammering them 4–1. Wayne was relegated to a substitute's role again and played no part in the match.

Dušan Tadić put Southampton ahead after eighteen minutes when he held off Phil Jagielka to turn the ball past Pickford. The shot-shy Saints had only scored nine goals in twelve Premier games. The single bright spot for Everton came just on half-time, when Gylfi Sigurdsson equalised with a spectacular goal. It was a curious effort, because it actually hit the woodwork three times before crossing the line. The midfielder tried his luck from long range and his stupendous dipping drive smashed, first against the crossbar, then hit a

post and the crossbar again before dropping into the back
of the net. The travelling Everton fans celebrated wildly. It
had been fifteen games since they had last won away and
perhaps this great goal would inspire them to victory.

Unsworth should have pitched Wayne on for the
second half and gone for a win, but Rooney stayed on the
bench. Sure, he had weakened his case for a recall with
his mediocre performance in the last game but the stats
indicated that no player had scored more Premier away
goals than him. The Saints' old-fashioned striker, Charlie
Austin, scored with two headers to put the game beyond
them, and he had not scored a Premier goal in almost a
year. He had scored the winner against the Toffees on the
same ground, 364 days previously.

Near the end of the game, Steven Davis completed the
rout with an angled drive past Pickford. Everton's ponderous
defence had now conceded nine goals in four days and
Unsworth's charges now stood two places above the bottom
three. Steve Claridge, covering the game for Radio 5 live,
commented as Everton were crushed that, 'It was hard to
describe what we are seeing.'

The camera panned across to Rooney sitting on the
bench, visibly wincing as the goals cascaded in, watching
another hyper-turgid performance. Sitting this one out was
a wise move by Wayne, albeit unintentionally. With his
face glowering at us from the TV screen he looked like a
hollowed-out walnut. A genuine sadness had overtaken him
at the ineptitude that his team, his *beloved* Everton Football
Club, were displaying.

Or, as the wonderful lyrics of David Bowie's song 'Space Oddity' describe: 'Planet earth is blue and there's nothing we can do?'

In the talkSPORT interview with Alan Brazil, Wayne expressed the opinion that he thought Unsworth should have gone after the Atalanta game. The shattered Unsworth faced the press to admit that, 'It's killing me.'

He went on to say that things must change. And he got his wish.

The next day he was relieved of his post and it was announced that Sam Allardyce would take charge at Goodison. The former England boss was enjoying a break in Dubai when he got the call that he had won his battle to obtain a two-and-a-half-year deal, worth around £100k a week.

Things were about to get lively.

CHAPTER 14

THE HUNGER GAMES

'After that incredible first goal against Arsenal, when
Arsène Wenger was talking to the world's media about
his special talent, Wayne was already out on his BMX
bike, meeting his mates outside the local chip shop.
He even ended up kicking a ball with them.'
PAUL STRETFORD, ROONEY'S AGENT

WINTER 2002

Wayne's hopes of winning a medal in the Worthington
Cup ended with a 1–4 defeat at the hands of Chelsea
at Stamford Bridge. Both teams fielded strong line-ups with
Wayne being handed his fifth start of the season. It might be
interesting to compare the line-ups:

CHELSEA
Cudicini, Melchiot, Babayaro, Gallas, Terry,

Lampard, Stanić (Morris 72), Petit, Gronkjaer
(De Lucas 64), Zola (Gudjohnsen 58), Hasselbaink

EVERTON
Wright, Pistone, Rhino, Weir, Yobo, Pembridge
(Naysmith 36), Li Tie (Gemmill 70), Gravesen,
Campbell, Radzinski, Rooney

The Toffees started brightly and Pembridge missed an
easy chance. Then the best thing to come out of Italy since
Sanpellegrino took over the team: Gianfranco Zola. After
twenty-five minutes Frank Lampard picked out the little
magician who spotted the run of Jimmy Floyd Hasselbaink
and he played a pass into the striker's path. The Dutchman
clipped the ball home instantly.

Wayne's first real contribution to the game came shortly
afterwards when he created a chance for Kevin Campbell
with a towering lob into the penalty area. For once though,
Rooney's strike partner failed to convert when he headed
straight at the Chelsea keeper, Carlo Cudicini.

Just before the break Zola chipped a neat pass to
Emmanuel Petit, who eluded the offside trap to volley past
Wright. (The Evertonians used to sing an amusing song
about the ex-Barca man Petit, referring to the fact of his
name being a porno film.)

The second half was one-sided as Chelsea pummelled
the Toffees, who had switched to a 4–2–4 formation. Zola
netted but was ruled offside and the Everton defence were
pleased to see him go off soon after. At that point in time

Chelsea were managed by the shrewd Claudio Ranieri. Conscious of a return match against Everton on Saturday he wanted to conserve Zola's energy.

Chelsea wrapped it up when Mario Stanić rose above Li Tie to head home Hasselbaink's corner, Chelsea's first corner of the game. Everton's defence was looking very flat and slow and it was no surprise when Hasselbaink scored the fourth. This was after his corner had been only partially cleared and he belted it home from a narrow angle.

Rooney had a chance to score when Gallas headed the ball virtually into his own hands and a penalty was awarded. Up stepped the boy from Crocky, hoping to register his first penalty kick in the big time. It was an important moment for him and he hit the ball hard enough but Cudicini, who had replaced Mark Bosnich, made a flying save to turn the ball around the post. Wayne was bitterly disappointed at his miss but was consoled when, from the ensuing corner, slack marking by John Terry allowed space for Naysmith to prod home from close range. I do not know if this could be put down as an assist.

Three days later, in another of those fixture quirks, Chelsea travelled to Goodison and won a tense battle 3–1. It was an interesting time for the West London club. The following summer Roman Abramovich was to turn up with his billions and rewrite their history and that of English football. In seven seasons Chelsea had never finished out of the top six. They had twice won the Cup and also won the Cup Winners Cup and yet the club was £80 million in debt. That season though, they were to qualify for the

Champions League and two pillars of the dynasty that were to scoop so many honours – Terry and Lampard – were already in place.

Everton were very committed that day, determined to avenge their defeat. After giving away two sloppy first-half goals the Toffees dominated the second half but Rhino was sent off and their chances of salvaging something from the game went with him. Rhino walked after a clash with the Chelsea winger Gronkjaer, who received a booking for his part in the fracas. Feelings ran high and Moyes had to restrain Unsworth from continuing the dispute with the Chelsea winger.

Everton returned to winning ways with a 2–1 victory over Blackburn Rovers at Goodison the following week. Wayne, putting aside the disappointments of the Chelsea defeats, was the Man of the Match, setting up the equaliser and scoring the winner. Another master striker had put Blackburn in front though, and this was Andrew Cole as he had decided to call himself. I remember him when he used to go by the name of Andy, and once scored five goals for Manchester United against Ipswich.

Cole's early goal for Blackburn was set up for him by another boyhood blue, David Thompson. In a breathless start, Lee Carsley scored the equaliser and began the move by finding Wayne on the edge of the box. The player in the Number 18 shirt with the hair-trigger responses took vicious aim and sent in a low shot which hit the foot of the post. It bounced out to Carsley, whose conversion was a formality. After twenty-five minutes Goodison erupted when Wayne scored a dazzling goal. Latching onto a hefty clearance by keeper Wright, he flicked it on, beating Blackburn defender Craig Short for sheer pace and lashing home what turned out to be the winning goal. Wayne had the instincts of a shark: when he smelt blood, he went for the kill. All of Rooney's goals so far had proved to be match winners.

Blackburn were managed by Graham Souness, a particular foe of the Everton crowd because of his antics for Liverpool as both a player and manager. To put one over on him was always a great crowd pleaser. Once again Wayne was lauded in the press; it seemed that the emergence of a talent such as his generated a strange kind of hysteria, the man-boy status was a constant reference point. The ex-Arsenal manager, George Graham, had famously quipped after his celebrated goal against his old club, 'Wayne Rooney has a man's body on a teenager's head.'

The freakish strength of the precocious youngster was of great interest to the media, and his outrageous skill, terrific shooting skills and powerful running made him the next superstar in the making. At that stage in his career, every time he walked off the field unable to say he was the best player on it, Moyes could have said to him that he had failed.

Wayne was represented as a feral, elfin figure: a cross between Fred Flintstone and Mozart. Wolfgang Amadeus Mozart had displayed prodigious musical ability from his earliest childhood, writing his first sonata at the age of five and his first symphony at eight. The cause of his death at thirty-five was never really determined and he was buried in a common grave. In contrast, Wayne Rooney at the end of this story was living in a mansion worth £20 million.

The only person that could have derailed Wayne's journey to the stratosphere of world football was himself. He had to stay dedicated, stay out of trouble, stay on the training ground. The modern game is full of cautionary tales. The archetype of failed 'next big things' was Jermaine Pennant, who was once seen to be as big a sensation as Wayne was at this juncture. Pennant was signed for Arsenal by Arsène Wenger from Notts County for a record fee, and comparisons were made of him to the Brazilian icon, Garrincha. The final reasons for his failure to attain superstardom were varied and highly complex, including a lack of confidence, injury worries, and the stress of being under constant pressure. But lifestyle choices were the main reasons why he didn't achieve great things.

Wayne always maintained that the greatest influence on his career was Colin Harvey, who had coached him in his formative years. Colin's words are documented in *Faith of Our Families: Everton FC, an Oral History*, by James Corbett (De Coubertin Books, 2017):

'I always used to go in early and I was going in about 6 a.m. one summer's morning. There were five kids crossing the road he was one of them. He did not see me I drove past. I phoned his dad and said "Come in with him."

'I said to him, "Do you want to be a footballer or don't you? If you're going to knock around with them, knock around with them, otherwise get yourself away from them and you have a chance of being a footballer."'

Wayne would always extol Harvey for pushing him hard as a youngster and instilling belief and confidence in him as a footballer. However, the fact that he kept him on the right path cannot be underestimated.

Three days before Christmas 2002 Everton travelled to Liverpool to Anfield. It was Wayne's first Merseyside Derby. The last time he had been on that historic pitch was when he was the Everton mascot and had 'lobbed' the ex-binman Neville Southall MBE. Southall used to say that Everton needed a strong Liverpool and Liverpool needed a strong Everton. He always contended that it was no good for anybody if just one team dominated the city.

The game ended in a 0–0 bore draw, one of the scrappiest inadequate encounters of that era. Liverpool had finished runners-up the previous season but at that time had lost their last four league games. They had a difficult season, on the last day of which Chelsea beat Liverpool to secure the fourth Champions League spot at their expense. The brightest moment of the game came after seventy-five minutes, when Wayne swivelled and fired in a strong shot, which deflected off Henchoz's leg and onto the bar. We have recently seen how a shot from Sigurdsson hit the woodwork three times before it was a goal, however in this match the ball came back out. It had all been down to angles, luck, millimetres.

In the usual double shuffle Wayne had come on for Radzinski after fifty-five minutes. His arrival was greeted with a storm of boos and caustic abuse from the home crowd and a huge cheer from the Evertonians. The teenager acquitted himself well and soon made his presence felt with a hefty challenge on the Liverpool keeper Chris Kirkland, which left him limping for the rest of the match. The big custodian had been the subject of a huge transfer from Coventry, and looked to have a long career in front of him as England's number one. But unfortunately injury and some inconsistent displays robbed him of that.

Michael Owen was in the Liverpool team that day and this gave the fans a chance to compare the Mersey sharpshooters. Owen had had a successful World Cup in Japan the previous summer, scoring against Denmark and Brazil and winning the fantastical penalty that defeated Argentina. He was eighteen months away from leaving Anfield to join Beckham at Real Madrid. In the following years, with Rooney already snapping at his heels, he eventually eclipsed his goal-scoring records for club and country. Owen had been one of Wayne's boyhood heroes, with his searing pace, coolness and unfathomable moves. Wayne's idolatry knew no bounds, and he had particular memories of watching on TV the goal Michael Owen had scored against Brazil. He'd been so excited by it that he had run out into the street, celebrating in the same manner and eager to thump the first football he saw. In his wildest imagination could he ever have thought that one day he would be re-enacting such scenarios for real on the world stage?

The game deteriorated into a series of ugly scuffles as the fouls thundered in and tempers frayed. David Weir and Kevin Campbell were booked and an unseemly melee occurred with Wayne in the middle of it, occurring after Steven Gerrard's two-footed tackle on Gary Naysmith. The veterans of the Merseyside derbies in the Everton squad would always tell Wayne what horribly nervous affairs these were. The banter was always more intense, the supporters just slagging off the opposing team's players. Danny Murphy took a lot of stick that day, a section of the crowd calling him 'Belsen Head', with Wayne playing up to the crowd's boos with the pluck of Widow Twanky.

It was not that happy a Christmas for Wayne. He spent Crimbo morning with Coleen, exchanging presents. Wayne bought her some jewellery, and amongst his presents was a giant box of the wine gums he still craved. They found time to watch his favourite film *Oliver!* based on the Lionel Bart musical, that was in turn based on the Dickens novel. I am sure that some wine gums were involved. Apart from being a world-class footballer, one of Wayne's main accomplishments was his assertion that he could sing every song in the *Oliver!* score. I can imagine him serenading Coleen with a rendition of the wonderful song, 'I'd Do Anything'. The line in it – 'paint your face bright blue' – would have had particular resonance for him.

Wayne identified strongly with the 'Artful Dodger' character in the film, who was head urchin of Fagin's gang of thieves, the cheeky young lad living on his wits, a youngster cast adrift in a tough, uncompromising world. The character in the film was played by Jack Wild, who had been discovered by a theatrical agent whilst playing football in the park. After the global success of the smash-hit film and an Academy Award nomination, Jack literally had the world at his feet as fame awaited him. At his peak he was receiving 2,000 fan letters a week. Like Wayne, the young actor married his childhood sweetheart. But after particular initial success in American TV his career tapered off and he became an alcoholic, beset by financial problems. Wild died from oral cancer at the age of fifty-three. His life served as a warning to Wayne.

On Boxing Day Everton travelled to St Andrews to play Birmingham. Once again Wayne started the game on the bench. He probably wished he had stayed there but Moyes sent him on near the end to break the deadlock, and the game finished 1–1. Once again, he was wound up tight and anxious to make something happen. A sliding tackle on the Brummie's defender Steve Vickers injured him sufficiently to warrant seven stitches. Wayne was adamant that though it was a hard tackle, he only went for the ball. Since he had first kicked a ball he had learnt to use his physique. That well-known pundit and award-winning podcaster Robbie Savage was playing for Birmingham that afternoon. He ran half the length of the pitch to the referee David Elleray to remonstrate about the tackle. The end result was that Rooney received the first red card of his career.

The Everton fans who had given up their Boxing Day

celebrations to travel to the Midlands were incensed. The story went that one particularly vocal Evertonian yelled out: 'Savage, you cheating, long-haired, gypsy Welsh c**t!'

Mark Pembridge, Welsh International, replied to him: 'Oi, Lar, less of the Welsh!'

Most nights Savage can be heard laying down the law on TV or the phone-ins, talking about all the hot topics of the day in the modern game. He covers a multitude of issues: diving, the rights and wrongs of the new VAR technology, players' wages, etc.

The problem was that Wayne had already received four yellow cards that season and his 'card' in the eyes of many officials was already marked. Most of all it was his sheer demeanour of aggression that did not serve him well on the field and made him an uneasy player to govern. Moyes defended Wayne as best he could, and today they could have replayed the tackle there and then tried to ascertain who was at fault. Eventually Elleray watched the video but the decision remained and Wayne had to sit out the next three matches.

Speaking of pundits, former Crystal Palace owner Simon Jordan, now working for talkSPORT, once famously described the controversial Elleray as: 'Going around with his arms folded like a schoolteacher. Which of course he is.'

A new year dawned: 2003. Concorde flew for the last time, Saddam Hussein was captured by the US Army and Johnny Cash died. Everton were tipped for the Cup by some experts, and were enjoying a much-improved season under their shrewd operator of a manager, who was fielding an experienced, well-drilled side. They also included the hottest property in the game – young Master Rooney. Comfortably placed in the League and with no European games to distract or disrupt them, they were considered a good bet to lift the trophy for the first time since 1995. With Paul Rideout's header beating Manchester United, Rhino was part of the Everton side.

The football gods must have smiled on them because they were handed what appeared to be an easy draw – away to Shrewsbury Town. This was a team lying seventh from the bottom of the Third Division (remember that?, who had preserved their status in the League with a win on the last day of the 1999/2000 season. The history of Everton Football Club is comprised of victories in games in which they were not given much chance and defeats in games that they should have won.

On the day, Shrewsbury put Everton out, winning 2–1. The game was watched by 7,800 at the quaintly named Gay Meadow on the banks of the River Severn (five years later, the club relocated to the re-christened New Meadow). To many people it was the biggest upset in the competition since my local team Sutton had beaten Coventry in 1989, two years after they had won the Cup by beating Tottenham. Wayne started the game and picked up another booking; the brevity of his fuse was giving Moyes cause for concern.

Shrewsbury were managed by Kevin Ratcliffe, one of Wayne senior's favourite players. Ratcliffe was Everton's most successful captain, leading them to the 2–0 victory over Watford in the 1984 Cup Final and winning the Premier

League and European Cup Winners' Cup the following year. Howard Kendall was always of the opinion that Ratcliffe's role in Everton's greatest team was overlooked. Whilst not the most technically gifted defender, he was fast and aggressive and, rare for today, he was brilliant on the left side. In the dressing room he ruled with a rod of iron.

Shrewsbury lay eighty places below Everton in the League, but only a string of fine saves by Richard Wright denied them in the early stages. The thirty-three-year-old striker, Nigel Jemson, was the match winner, and this was his twelfth club, his spell at Nottingham Forest being his most notable. Jemson put Shrewsbury ahead with a wonderful free kick, dipping and swerving over the wall after Gravesen had been booked for a nasty foul. Rooney was finding the going tough, singled out as he was for some heavy tackles and denied any space by the energetic Shrewsbury defenders. Kevin Campbell missed the game through injury and Wayne missed his strike partner, who had given him such valuable support and experience. He played too deep, as there was nobody to hold the ball up for him: with Campbell in the team he always knew where the ball was.

A furious Moyes read the riot act at half-time and Gravesen was replaced by Niclas Alexandersson, who equalised on the hour. It was a neat goal as he cut in to score with a low drive. Wayne burst into life and smashed in a shot from about twenty yards that just skimmed the crossbar, and the tie looked to be heading for a replay, which Rooney was looking forward to playing in. With a minute to go, Rhino conceded a free kick, which another ex-Forest player, Ian

Woan, floated over for Nigel Jemson to head home at the near post. In the first half Wright had made a fantastic save from an almost identical header by the same player, and this time he got a hand to it but could not keep it out.

Such is football. And so the fancied Everton side crashed out at the first hurdle. When the whistle blew for the end of the match, Shrewsbury's two-goal hero Jemson made a beeline for Wayne so he could swap shirts. I hope he has kept the shirt.

CHAPTER 15

RE-MAKE/RE-MODEL

'Wayne Rooney – he can play anywhere he wants.'
SAM ALLARDYCE, SPEAKING AS ENGLAND COACH

NOVEMBER/DECEMBER 2017

Of course the jury was out about the appointment of the big man. The purists were insisting that his style of football would not suit 'The People's Club', a club that had fielded the likes of Alex Young, The Ball-Kendall-Harvey axis, Kevin Sheedy, David Ginola, Duncan McKenzie and Pat Nevin to name a few. Everton were going back to the days of Gordon Lee; it would be all that long ball, playing for set pieces and grinding out results. Everton always got the ball forward quickly, rather than playing out from the back.

Big Sam has been likened to 'Red Adair', the American troubleshooter in the oil production industry, who specialised in the quenching of potentially disastrous, out-of-control oil fires. As for Allardyce, the sixty-three-year-old man's latest job had been saving Crystal Palace from almost certain relegation the previous season. There was even talk that Everton owed the South London club £1 million in compensation. Sam had wanted an incentive for keeping Everton in the Premier but the view from the boardroom was that the club did not pay for 'just survival'.

Of course, we had heard all the moans from the West Ham fans, who have similar pretensions and self-righteously claimed that when Allardyce was in charge he was not the man to produce football in the best traditions of their club. This was another 'self-styled school of science' which had the monopoly on playing this mythical football, which was a mixture of Cruyff's 'total football' Ajax side and the 1970 Brazil World Cup winning team.

I watched West Ham in the sixties and had the pleasure of seeing Bobby Moore, Martin Peters and Geoff Hurst. The salient point was that the other eight players in the side were not of the same standard. Harry Redknapp was one of those players, at best mediocre and the perpetual butt of the crowd because of his repeated failure to produce anything. Now we have him as one of the longest-serving managers in the game, a relic from the street mythology of the East End.

Even when West Ham had a player with the silky skills of Alan Devonshire in the team, circa season 85/86, when they finished third behind Everton, the spiky Billy Bonds was their most important player. Speaking of West Ham, they just happened to be Everton's opponents on the Wednesday night following Sam's arrival. By another remarkable twist of fate David Moyes was in charge of the Claret and Blues. Like Wayne, he had something to prove to the Goodison faithful. After eleven seasons what he had so carefully built lay in tatters after stints as Sir Alex Ferguson's kamikaze successor at Old Trafford and then at the train wreck that was Sunderland Football Club. Even Red Adair would have swerved that disaster area.

Moyes was slowly rehabilitating himself as one of football's leading managers, and the honesty and straightforward manner with which he met this latest challenge was to be admired. The Scot had been set up for the impossible when he tried to fill the shoes of Ferguson and rebuild an ailing, unbalanced team. Fast forward a couple of years through the failure of the inconsistent Louis Van era and even José Mourinho was finding it hard to achieve the domination that Ferguson had enjoyed for so long, a supremacy that Wayne Rooney had played no small part in establishing. After all, he was their all-time top scorer, a situation created by his cobra-style striking.

That week at the end of November both Everton and West Ham were stuck in some parallel universe of their own making. Both teams had delusions of grandeur before the season had started.

They envisaged being in the top six, with an outside chance of cracking the top floor if any of the big boys slipped up. Instead, both teams were in the bottom six with relegation and the carnage that entailed becoming a very realistic prospect. West Ham had sacked Slaven Bilić two weeks after Koeman had collected his P45, and had acted quickly in employing Moyes on a short-term contract until the end of the season. With Moyes you knew what you were getting: an experienced manager with proven ability at the highest level. Moyes was precisely that, and Everton had persevered with Rhino long after his cover had been blown.

Of course, not everyone agreed. Everton fan Mike Burke thought that, 'Unsworth should have been kept on and given more time. West Ham was a team that we always beat. Huddersfield was another game we could have obtained points from which would have lifted us up the table.'

For Wayne, though he probably did not appreciate it at the time, it was one of the most important games in his career. It was a chance to re-establish himself in the team and prove his worth to his new boss. The top teams now needed forward players with not only athleticism but the work rate required to press the opposition. At thirty-two, Rooney no longer had the engine to perform at that intense level for ninety minutes. Not that Allardyce needed any convincing of Wayne's ability, he had always been a fan.

When Allardyce was appointed as England coach the debate was still raging as to whether or not Rooney should be in the national team and if so, in what position. In the press conference after his only game in charge against Slovakia the question of Wayne came up. Allardyce looked surprised that he was even asked such a question. The answer was as had been quoted earlier: he declared that Rooney could play wherever he wanted to.

True to his word, Sam oversaw that Wayne was reinstated

in the team to play left of midfield and he made him captain. By this simple stroke of genius, he immediately won Wayne over and, almost as importantly, got the approval of sections of the crowd. In his last film appearance the late Oliver Reed advised Russell Crowe in *Gladiator* that to survive in the combat arenas he had to, 'Win the crowd.'

Everything pointed to an interesting match, but nobody could have guessed how fantastic an evening it turned out to be. After eighteen minutes Everton were awarded a penalty kick and Wayne elected to take it. It had been awarded in controversial circumstances. West Ham's Obiang mistimed a clearance which was sliced to Dominic Calvert-Lewin. Scarcely believing his good fortune, Dominic's instant pace took him away from Joe Hart, who pulled him down. Hart was another person drinking in the last chance saloon – it must have been crowded that night with Moyes, Allardyce and perhaps even Rooney in there. West Ham protested about the decision but in the absence of any VAR it stood. The ref decided that Calvert-Lewin would have scored if he had regained control of the ball. Hart actually saved Wayne's effort, not one of his best, on a par with his effort against Chelsea in the Worthington Cup that we discussed in the previous chapter. The ball looped up though, and Wayne's reactions were quicker than those of the 'Sundance Kid'. He jumped up to head the ball over the sprawling Hart and into the net.

Ten minutes later he scored his and Everton's second goal. Jonjoe Kenny mis-kicked Tom Davies's cross and the ball skidded into the path of Rooney, who slammed it first time past Hart. West Ham came out fighting in the second half. Their performance in the first half had been as abysmal as Everton's performance at Southampton, a match now being dubbed as 'The St Mary's Day Massacre' by the fans. Moyes's team had their first shot in the fifty-second minute when Lanzini forced Pickford to make his first save of the night. The stats indicate that this was the third-longest wait by a team in the Premier to make an attempt on goal. Creswell hit the Everton bar from the rebound and then Ashley Williams gave away a penalty. Pickford saved Lanzini's kick, and it was the first match in the Premier for three years that both sides missed a penalty. (That was Man City v Spurs in October 2014 in case you are interested.) Just when it looked like Moyes's men were getting back into the goal, Wayne conjured a strike that was straight out of his bumper book of golden, all-time great goals.

It is a well-known fact that Wayne is a great fan of Harry Potter. He has read all the books about the bespectacled boy wizard and seen the films. I am a 'Rooneyista', and I always believed that there was a 'metaphysical and mystery' aspect to his football. A Spanish sports newspaper, *Diario AS*, ran a headline during the 2004 Euros stating that: 'Wayne Rooney is the new Harry Potter'.

With his magic tricks and nose for the ball, the Spanish journalists saw him as the 'bestseller' of the competition.

Football is the most superstitious business in the world. Most players always take their first step onto the pitch with their right foot. And every player had his own dressing room superstition. Wayne's particular one was that he would always put on his shirt sitting on the bench in one particular place, then he would put on his socks and boots in another favoured spot.

José Mourinho's first game in charge for Real Madrid was against Mallorca. Having just won the Champions League with Inter Milan the levels of expectation were sky high. When the game ended in a dull 0–0 draw, Wayne's old boss was quick to point out he was a coach and not a magician; indeed, he was no Harry Potter.

There was no doubt that the third goal that he scored that night against West Ham was like something out of the pages of the JK Rowling books. It started with Hart rushing from his goal to clear another desperate situation. The ball found Wayne, who was four yards inside his OWN half. He drilled the ball over the heads of two back-tracking Hammers defenders and with Hart stranded, the ball flew into the net. Rooney's comprehension of the positioning of Hart and the two helpless defenders was instant. The economy of his back lift allowed him to instantly produce powerful shots in the tightest of situations. The goal was a personal statement and a beautifully constructed vindication of his return to the Everton fold.

Like golfer Tommy Fleetwood with a nine-iron in his hand, he had executed the perfect long-range chip. (Incidentally, Tommy is a staunch Evertonian and a rising star in the world of golf, and he follows the Toffees wherever he is in the world.) The fact that it brought Wayne his first trio in a blue shirt was almost incidental. The goal was totally remarkable and will live in the memory of all who saw it.

That ability to propel the ball over opponents was always an important facet of his game.

Only a handful of truly great players possess the vision, skill and the power to harness such a situation for a direct goal attempt. Coaches would claim that the ball would travel through the air too slowly and that the margin of error is too great. In a game driven by data, the algorithms are confounded by idiosyncratic talents such as Wayne's, who embody the true arts of football and whose sheer audacity knows no bounds.

Portrayed by many as a dullard with no social skills, a Scally kid from Croxteth and the opposite of a role model, this goal demonstrated precisely how intelligent a player he was. The only English player who displayed similar nous and sublime cheek in the last twenty-five years is another Scally, this time from Toxteth: Robbie Fowler.

The shot was hit from 57.67 yards with a velocity of 52.5 mph, and it won the BBC *Match of the Day* goal-of-the-month competition. It polled over 40 per cent of the vote in a strong month, beating a beautifully struck shot by the Liverpool striker Salah. As actor Al Pacino stated when he lined up a shot on a pool table in the film *Carlito's Way*: 'You are going to give up your religious beliefs after you have seen this shot.'

It was Wayne's first hat-trick for the Toffees, and his magnificent seventh in the Premier League, putting him one behind Thierry Henry and Michael Owen, who were on eight apiece. Robbie (Fowler) had nine. Speaking of *Match of the Day*, the programme's chief honcho, Alan Shearer, was out in front with eleven Premier hat-tricks. (Jimmy Greaves scored six hat-tricks in one season for Chelsea in 1960/61.)

It was 2,272 days since Rooney's last hat-trick for Manchester United in September 2011.

Allardyce watched the game from the directors' box, sitting next to Farhad Moshiri. Earlier in the day they had finalised the latter's deal at Finch Farm. Both men jumped to their feet when Wayne sealed his hat-trick, and raised their thumbs. The Iranian investor was watching the template of an 'Allardyce survival kit': an organised defence, a hard-working aggressive midfield and ruthless counter-attacking. Sam had never underestimated Wayne's toughness or his outstanding talent. At Bolton he had extracted every last ounce of effort and skill from his ageing players by keeping them razor-sharp and treating them with the utmost respect.

Talking to *The Sun*, Wayne described his third goal thus:

> I don't think I have scored better.
> It was as good as I have ever kicked a football. For it to earn my first hat-trick for Everton, I am delighted.
> It's also my first goal in front of the Gwladys Stand since I have been back and I have been desperate to do that.

A late header by Williams from Gylfi Sigurdsson's cross made it 4–0 but it was irrelevant, as the game was over with Wayne's third goal. So how did Moyes feel at the end of the game, watching his erstwhile prodigy wreak havoc on his new team? It was a tad surreal. It was Moyes's fifth loss at the hands of Everton, having lost two apiece previously with Manchester United and Sunderland. As we have seen, it was on Moyes's watch that Wayne launched his incredible career. Yet the two men as protagonists in a classical Greek tragedy fell out eventually in his first spell at Everton only to link up again at Old Trafford.

To prosper in top-class football, or just to withstand the pressure, both men had to possess some sterner aspects: lack of compromise and single-minded determination amongst them. The psychological relationship they enjoyed was extremely complex, rather like the Brothers Gallagher of Oasis, alternating over the years between protection and alienation, secrecy and revelation, love and irritation.

Moyes also spoke to *The Sun* at the end of the match, a sombre undercurrent flowing beneath the spin, percolating the surface of his words. He said: 'We did not deserve that score. Everton's penalty changes it, it's poor defending. But very few players could have done what Rooney did for his third. It was terrific.'

Rhino milked the applause at the end and patted the badge. Then he disappeared down the tunnel, facing the anonymity of the Academy.

The newspapers went overboard with their treatment of the game, establishing Wayne as a superstar again in the eyes of the public. Samples of their pun-related references to Rooney are:

'Have Sam of that'.

'Rooney has three rein'

'HEROO'

The press were not so lavish in their praise of Sam. Some were going with the suggestion that he was the back-up guy when the move for Marco Silva crashed and burnt. Allardyce, however, was insisting his credentials for the biggest club job of his career were 'incomparable' to Silva's. The ex-Limerick player-manager made a passing reference to Hull's relegation under Silva's stewardship, and that he thought that Everton wanted to give the job to Unsworth first and foremost, before him or the Watford coach at that time.

The following Saturday Huddersfield Town came to Goodison. Newly promoted, they had done reasonably well at that stage considering the limited resources that they had available. Wayne was in the side, boosted by his mid-week exploits against West Ham. A healthy crowd of 39,167 turned up on a cold afternoon a few weeks away from Christmas. The first half was deadly dull, with Huddersfield having more of the ball but lacking the penetration to make anything of it. They had not scored an away goal since the first day of the season and rarely threatened. So far in fifteen League games, Everton had conceded twenty-eight goals, the third worst figures in that League. A constant changing of the personnel in the back four (which sometimes was a back five) had added to their problems.

Big Sam was prowling the touchline, in a heavy, dark winter coat. The fans were joking that the club was saving money by hiring him because he was the only manager who could fit into Rhino's old club suit and trackies. It was his seventh job in the Premier, one more than Alan Pardew and two more than Messrs Redknapps and Hodgson. He blamed his new club's poor display in the first half on fatigue from their recent run of fixtures.

Sam did not mind if his side did not dominate possession. Roberto Martinez had been obsessed by this facet of the game, and his successor, Koeman, took a similar view. Martinez always struggled to win over the Evertonians, who quickly ran out of patience with his slower style, particularly when the results went against him. In the whole match they only had 44 per cent possession, and against Moyes's Hammers they had an identical amount of the ball.

Everton attacked from the start of the second half and Calvert-Lewin neatly back-heeled to Sigurdsson to slide home. The goal settled the home side down and Calvert-Lewin should have added a second from a good position but dallied too long on the ball and was dispossessed before he could score. In the next minute though, Wayne sent a chillingly accurate pass to the same player, who galloped through to score the second. Dominic's willingness to keep going took him into shooting positions and this time his killing shot worked. With ten minutes left, Sam took Wayne off to be replaced by Michael Keane. So far so good with the new boss.

Six goals had been scored and none conceded.

CHAPTER 16

THIS IS ENGLAND 2003

'I don't need to tell him how to score goals.'
SVEN-GÖRAN ERIKSSON, ON ROONEY'S FIRST ENGLAND CAP

'One of the best mixers, one of the people that moved
easily between the different cliques was Wayne Rooney.
He is such an easy bloke to get along with and he is
popular with everybody.'
Theo: Growing Up Fast by Theo Walcott (Bantam, 2011),
describing his time in the England camp for the 2010
World Cup

After the humiliating Cup exit at Gay Meadow, Rooney
was suspended following his red card at Birmingham.
He was eligible to play again at the Valley in a fixture
against Charlton Athletic in early February 2003. One cold
morning a few days before the match he was preparing to

start training at Bellefield when David Moyes motioned him over. His first thoughts were, 'What have I done now?'

The relationship between the two had been rather strained of late. Wayne had missed games because of his sending off, and also because of an incident that involved his appearance at the BBC Sports Personality of the Year Awards. Rooney had been nominated and correctly won the Young Sports Personality of the Year Award 2002. It showed the esteem that he was held in and how quickly the public had latched onto this 'Roy of the Rovers' from Merseyside.

Wayne wanted to take Coleen down to London to collect his award. He had been booked into a five-star top-rank hotel, with the full red-carpet treatment. The event was being televised live on BBC One on a Sunday night. It was to be the start of the Yellow Brick Road for the young couple. Moyes put the kibosh on this plan to bring Coleen to London for reasons that were unclear to Wayne.

At the ceremony, Wayne apparently let himself down by committing the heinous crimes of chewing gum and appearing with his tie undone. Really! Had he consulted *How to Be a Gentleman Revised and Updated: A Contemporary Guide to Common Courtesy* by John Bridges (Thomas Nelson, 2012), he would have assumed that black tie is appropriate for any formal event commencing after seven. The press, as he was to find out over the years, turned on him like a pack of wolves.

Wayne was never a clothes horse. Despite his huge personal fortune his own appearance was never of great importance to him. With a hairstyle more famous than Angelina Jolie's right leg, he always favours low-key sportswear, such as

Nike sweaters. Wayne always maintained that he had been hot under the blazing lights and had loosened his tie. And he chewed because he wanted his breath to be sweet.

It seemed a long time since that sunny afternoon when Robert Chelsea Moore, captain of England, wiped his muddy hands on the cloth covering the presentation area. This was before shaking hands with Her Majesty the Queen, when she presented him with the Jules Rimet trophy.

Moyes was all smiles on that day and congratulated Rooney on being called up for England. Wayne thought he was referring to a spot in the England Under-21 squad. In the natural progression of things that was his next stage of development. The plan was to establish himself in that team and then try to emulate Franny Jeffers's total haul of thirteen goals in thirteen games for the Under-21s. A sprightly Franny had made his debut for Everton in 1997, also at the age of sixteen – Wayne had beaten him by thirty-eight days.

Delighted at the news of being called up for England, Wayne asked Moyes if Tony Hibbert had been called up with him.

A surprised Moyes shook his head and told him that Wayne's friend was in the Under-21 team. Slowly it dawned on the young Englishman that he was going to be in the full squad. He was not even sure who they would actually be playing. It took a while for it to sink in. After training, his teammates presented him with a carton of milk in honour of his call-up. It was a running joke amongst the squad that every time Wayne scored a goal or received some award, they presented him with a carton of milk. After all, he was a growing lad and not man enough to drink yet. Rhino suggested that Mrs Rooney should write a note for him to stay up late, since the kick-off was past his usual bedtime.

Michael Owen was England's youngest player of the last century when he made his senior debut against Chile in February 1998 at the age of eighteen years and fifty-nine days. Three months later a goal against Morocco made him his country's youngest goal-scorer. The arrival of Rooney echoed that of Owen's bursting on the scene with a Merseyside team. The Everton starlet was on a remarkable trajectory with just a handful of first-team appearances and five goals. Wayne had not even been aware that Sven-Göran Eriksson had been closely monitoring his meteoric rise. The media might have accused Sven of being a timid manager, but he was not afraid to gamble with obvious talents like Wayne Rooney. Strangely, Sven had never been to see him play. The England coach was aware of Wayne's many qualities and now he was anxious to see if he could reproduce them at International level at such a young age.

Before the circus of England though, there was the Charlton match and Moyes kept Wayne on the bench until six minutes from time. Charlton had just scored to go 2–1 up and the new England call-up was introduced at the expense of Rhino. It was a late attempt by Moyes to try and save the game. Rooney almost did, with a beautifully struck shot which whistled just over the bar. It was not to be though, and the Toffees lost a game they should have taken something from.

THIS IS ENGLAND 2003

Uncle Eugene drove Wayne down to London so that he could join up with the England party. It must have been a great feeling for the older man, maybe it all started when he gave his nephew the leather ball. How many thousands of miles had he driven the youngster to training sessions and junior matches? And now he was going to the big one. When Wayne walked into the restaurant for the team match it was like a Panini sticker album that had come alive. They were all there, the golden generation of Beckham, Scholes and Lampard.

One of the biggest names of them all, Steven Gerrard, came over to introduce himself to the new boy. It was like his first day at Our Lady and St Swithin's Roman Catholic primary school. The fact that Gerrard took time out to make Wayne feel at home showed just what class and decency he had. The two men had played against each other in the score-less Mersey derby about six weeks ago, but this was the first time that they had met up off the pitch.

Steven's cousin Anthony Gerrard was in the same year of the Everton School of Excellence that Wayne had played in. Anthony was good enough to have signed professional forms for Everton but had never made the first team and had moved to Walsall. Wayne, who had shared the substitute's bench with Anthony, enquired after him and the ice was broken with Steven.

Since he retired Gerrard has never really received the accolades he deserved. The press runs stories about him presenting his six-year-old daughter with 18-carat rose gold iPads worth £1,500, but the point was missed. At his peak he was the most complete English midfielder of his era, just as Rooney was the most complete striker. His influence on the DNA of English players such as Wayne cannot be underestimated.

It was also a chance for Wayne to meet up with his old friend Franny Jeffers, who had joined Arsenal in June 2001. He had started 2000/01 brightly, but his season crumbled under a succession of ankle and shoulder injuries. Arsène Wenger, a wonderful judge of players, had been tracking Jeffers's progress for some time and signed him for £8 million with another £2 million in extras. It was money Everton could not refuse at that time and it kept them afloat. Kevin Campbell had struck up a prolific partnership with Jeffers, as he did with Wayne, and was sorry to see him go. He had watched both players come up through the ranks and was aware that they were the lifeblood of the club. Selling them was like parting with the family silver.

Mike Burke had followed both their careers with interest and commented that, 'They were both Evertonians but there is no comparison between them as players. Jeffers was what I call a lucky striker in that he had a habit of scoring fortunate goals. Wayne? Well, he was just phenomenal.'

Franny Jeffers joined Steve and his new chum and soon the three young Scouse men were nattering away about the environment that had nurtured them. In an interview with *The Independent* Franny expanded on the point:

> When I was nine or ten, my mum had to come to search for me in the streets. You see, kids now they

come home from school, they are on the computers.
I would find people who were playing football.
Wayne grew up in Crocky. Everyone was doing it.
You would see little pockets of lads everywhere. It is
a bit different. The world has changed.

The next morning the two chaps from Croxteth went
shopping up West with another Scouser, Danny Murphy.
Danny, now an analyst (and, at times, professional Chelsea
cheerleader) on *Match of the Day*, could do with another
shopping trip judging by the state of his attire on a Saturday
evening. It is not known how many packs of Juicy Fruit
Wayne consumed or if he purchased any ties from Selfridges.

Another test for Rooney to overcome was with Gary
Neville. They had history from an early reserve game when
United visited Everton. Gary was already established in
the first team and was disliked on Merseyside by both the
red and blue sides for his comments about Scousers. The
coaching staff at Everton were anxious to see how tough
Wayne really was when he came up against a player of
Neville's stature. Early in the match they clashed. Gary took
an elbow in what Wayne claimed was an accident. Later in
the game Neville whacked the Everton starlet.

The face-off went okay but the dialogue was more
diplomatic than anything. Neville claimed that his anti-
Scouse comments were taken out of context. (A riff the
Neville boys were to repeat over the years.) What their
comments were aimed at was the Liverpool team of the
eighties that had dominated for so long. The team of

Souness, Rush, Hansen and Lawrenson. Wayne, being a staunch Evertonian, could relate to this.

That was also the first time Rooney met up with Owen Hargreaves, who was already an established star with Bayern Munich, having won the European Under-21 Player of the Year award in 2001. The same year he had helped them win the Champions League. Little did Wayne guess that he would be playing alongside him when he won a second Champions League medal with United. With his mop of dark curly hair and Mediterranean good looks, Owen was already attracting attention.

In the evening the England game was played at Upton Park. By this time Wayne had ascertained that their opponents were Australia. Sven had a squad of twenty-six players he used over the two halves. It was set out in the following manner:

FIRST HALF	SECOND HALF
David James	Paul Robinson
Gary Neville	Ledley King
Sol Campbell	Owen Hargreaves
Rio Ferdinand	Darius Vassell
Kieron Dyer	Paul Konchesky
David Beckham	Francis Jeffers
Michael Owen	Danny Mills
Paul Scholes	Danny Murphy
Frank Lampard	Jermaine Jenas
Wes Brown	Wayne Rooney
Ashley Cole	James Beattie

Amongst the subs were Everton's goalkeeper
Richard Wright and a young Joe Cole.

In the first half the English team 'stunk the gaffe out', as
Joey Barton would say, and went in at the break 0–2 down.
For the first goal Gary Neville could not deal with the burly
Popovic, who had arms like a California surfer, and the
defender bundled the ball home. The second goal was a basic
error by Frank Lampard, who lost the ball to Harry Kewell,
who was to Australian football what Shane Warne was to
their cricket team. Kewell spun Rio then walked around
David James to score with ease. Harry boy was another
player who should have been as big as Beckham. With his
pop-star looks he could have been the doppelgänger of the
lead singer of The Easybeats – Australia's biggest beat group
in the sixties, who, like Harry, ultimately failed to enjoy
sustained global success. As Marlon Brando once famously
mumbled, he could have 'been a contender', but injuries
disrupted his spells at Leeds and Liverpool. That night he
was unplayable.

As the England team left the pitch the announcer advised
that a completely different team would be appearing for the
second half. Ironic cheers broke out amongst the England
fans in the ground, who were heavily outnumbered by a
huge contingent that had turned up to follow Australia.
(Earls Court, the habitual hangout for ex-pat Aussies in
London, must have been empty that night.) The crowd
were watching history being made when Wayne Rooney
entered the fray. At seventeen years 111 days he was the

youngest player to be part of the full England team. The existing record had been set in 1879 by James Prinsep of Clapham Rovers (you must remember them!), who was a mere seventeen years 253 days old when he was called up to play against Scotland.

The record lasted for 124 years, and James from Clapham Rovers only played the once for England. Research indicates that he was a real character, and he set another record as the youngest player to appear in a FA Cup Final. That was Rovers' 0–1 defeat to the toffs that called themselves the Old Etonians – I must get the DVD of that game out! Sadly, James Prinsep died at the age of thirty-four from pneumonia, caught when he was playing golf.

Perhaps the youngster with the greatest potential ever was Duncan Edwards. He was eighteen years and 184 days old when he made his debut for England. Edwards was killed in the Munich air disaster of 1958, and was a player who encapsulated the tragedy of that period. It could make you weep.

That record was to be broken by Theo Walcott, who beat Rooney by thirty-six days. It was ironic that Theo, now twenty-eight, was to join Wayne at Everton in January 2018 from Arsenal. It was an attempt by Theo to kick-start his England career after winning forty-seven caps. It was on Wayne's recommendation that Theo signed for Sam Allardyce. Theo told *The Sun*: 'I played a lot of football with Wayne Rooney and I just wanted to get a structure of how the club worked. I got a sense from Wayne, he was hungry, eager to push on. He felt like it was the right place.'

As the singer-songwriter Bob Dylan observes – the media were always creating new idols, then crushing them. Wayne must have felt some empathy with Theo, since they were both prodigies having some distant dream of super-stardom, and both had been caught like a deer in the headlights. The difference between the two was that when Wayne made his England debut he was fully developed and as strong as an ox, whereas Theo was still growing when he burst onto the scene. When Theo scored three times in Zagreb against Croatia in a World Cup qualifying tie, the game that really defined his England career, Wayne had created all three goals.

Wayne was one of the five new players who had won their first caps that night at Upton Park. Sven had created another record by doing that. The new 'improved' England showed better form in the second half and pulled a goal back. Wayne played his part in it, finding Jermaine Jenas, who delivered an accurate cross for Franny Jeffers to head home his first and only goal for the full national side. It was a wonderful moment for the two lads from Crocky, combining their talents to score an absolute corker of a goal for their country at the highest level. Two sides of the same coin.

They were a tribute to the coaching staff at Bellefield and also to their old school, De La Salle (now an Academy). Two coaches had travelled down to London for the game, one containing the Rooney and Jeffers families and the other one teachers, students and alumni from their old school. Nobody was more aware than Wayne of how youngsters in

Croxteth could be dispossessed by growing up in a teenage wasteland. He was very keen to create a scholarship in his name to benefit a child from a disadvantaged background.

Australia put a slight damper on proceedings though, by scoring a late third goal through Brett Emerson, catching England on the counter. The Aussies in the crowd turned Upton Park into the 'Gabba' (The Brisbane Cricket Ground, a major sports stadium) that night, as they celebrated trouncing the Poms. I am not sure how much sledging went on. So, Wayne's first game ended in defeat but he had made an encouraging start. Jeffers was included in the next squad for the Euro 2004 qualifiers against Liechtenstein and Turkey, but Sven told him that he had not made the bench and dropped him down to the Under-21s. That was the only full cap he won.

Wayne was about to enter the digital shimmer of stardom. He was chosen for the Liechtenstein game and came on as a late sub for Emile Heskey with England 2–0 up. Although having had the briefest of cameos, Wayne received some more positive reviews for his pin-sharp, adrenalin-pumping appearance. By now it was clear that there was a lobby in the press to install him in the side. He was so close he could almost smell the fame.

Franny had scored for the Under-21s and returned to Liverpool to be with his parents. He was playing golf when his phone rang and it turned out to be his chum Wayne telling him that he was starting for the first time against Turkey. England won 2–0 and although Wayne did not score, he was named Man of the Match. I wonder what

Jeffers thought as he watched the game on TV. What was the title of that famous old Yvonne Fair soul record? Oh yes, 'It Should Have Been Me'.

Franny admitted that Wayne had been brilliant in that game. In an article in *The Independent* he stressed that: 'For me, based on stats, he is the greatest English striker of all time. On your goals alone. Ability-wise he probably is anyway because he can do everything.'

The first of Wayne's England goals came in September of that year against Macedonia in a European Championship qualifier. The game did not start well and at half-time England were trailing. Michael Owen had partnered Rooney up front but the duo could make little impression on the home defence. Sven decided to bring Emile Heskey on for Lampard to beef up the attack and dropped Wayne in behind them. Sven was experimenting with the diamond formation at that time, which was then very much in vogue. The result was like putting paraffin in a Rolls-Royce. Soon Wayne adapted to playing at the top of it; he was so adaptable, and as long as he played, he did not mind where.

After fifty-three minutes David Beckham's lofted pass was headed down by Emile Heskey and from the edge of the box Wayne shot low. It was not a particularly hard shot, in fact he had failed to connect properly, but the goalkeeper went down late and the ball ended up in the net. It was enough to make him England's youngest ever goal-scorer at the age of seventeen years and 317 days. His partner Michael Owen was the first to congratulate him on beating his record. Beckham got the winner from the penalty spot.

WAYNE ROONEY

A few days later England played Liechtenstein at Old Trafford in the second qualifier. Michael Owen put England ahead in the first minute of the second half. Wayne added a second six minutes later to score his first International goal on home soil. Joe Cole replaced him after sixty-seven minutes.

Football is just stats now, perhaps it always was. Reduced to: how many days? How many goals? How many passes?

But Wayne Rooney's stats were always the best.

CHAPTER 17

PURPLE WAYNE

'He is still a fantastic player and he has shown that.
I am not sure if it's allowed but I like Wayne Rooney as
a person. I have always liked him as a player.'
JÜRGEN KLOPP

DECEMBER 2017

Everton's next fixture was the away match against Apollon Limassol, the deadest of dead rubbers (meaning that this one result not affecting their overall position). It was a good chance to bring in some of the ingénues and squad players. Craig Shakespeare oversaw the easy 3–0 victory in Nicosia; a pre-arranged medical appointment meant Big Sam missed the game. Wayne was spared the 4,000 miles round trip and remained at home, keeping fit and repaying his debt to society at the Community Centre.

Ademola Lookman was the hero of the match, scoring twice

in a seven-minute spell in the first half. Signed from Charlton, he looked a real prospect as he peppered the Limassol goal. The following month he was sent out on loan to RB Leipzig, the Bundesliga club. He scored on his debut against Borussia Mönchengladbach, and was the first Englishman to score in that League since Owen Hargreaves in 2005. Vlasić scored the third, eight minutes from time with a low drive.

The biggie was coming up: a crucial game versus Liverpool at Anfield, the first time Wayne had played there since his return to the city. Everton had a poor record against Liverpool: they had not beaten them since 2010. The last time they had won at Anfield was September 1999 when Kevin Campbell had hit the winner. It was a difficult time to play them as they were coming off the back of a 7–0 victory over Spartak Moscow in the Champions League. Liverpool had a new Fab-Four to replace the original mop-tops: Mohamed Salah, Sadio Mané, Roberto Firmino and the quixotic Philippe Coutinho. The latter had scored a hat-trick against Spartak but was slowly edging to the door, lured by the magic of Barca and all that involved.

Liverpool were unbeaten in their last fourteen derby clashes and were keen to beat the total of fifteen set by their superteam in the 1970s. Sam Allardyce had already tasted victory at Anfield in the calendar year when he had led the team he was then managing, Crystal Palace, to a wonderfully controlled 2–1 victory. Wayne was determined to get something from the game. At this stage in his galactic career what with his vast experience and his Evertonian idealism, he was seen as a calming influence in the team.

PURPLE WAYNE

When Wayne had finally left Old Trafford he accepted that his days of winning major honours on a regular basis had passed him by. What he had moved to Everton for was days like this, the Merseyside game being one of the biggest derbies in world football. Anfield held no terrors for him, nothing could have been so intimidating as his first appearance as a mascot there. Whilst playing for United he had twice scored the winner. As always, nothing fazed him, he was staggeringly assured. In his first spell at Everton he had failed to score against his bitterest rivals. At United he had scored a total of six goals in twenty-five games against them.

When at the start of the season he was asked what team he was most looking forward to playing against he answered instantly, 'Liverpool.'

How he must have longed to have scored against his bitterest foes whilst wearing an Everton shirt! Allardyce was counting on Wayne to do something special and wanted him to call upon the experience he had gained with United in their brutal battles with Liverpool. He told the *Daily Star* in his usual erudite manner: 'As an Evertonian he is desperate to do well. As he was when he was at Manchester United and desperate to beat them then. Everton is his club and he can use all that experience to deliver the kind of performance he gave against West Ham.'

It was a freezing late afternoon when the Mersey giants met, and snowflakes fell on the Kop just before the game kicked off. Their traditional anthem 'You'll Never Walk Alone' was played and the crowd sang along, bathed in its sepia glow. It was said that Bill Shankly regarded the Kop's version of the song as the true sound of the City of Liverpool, not The Beatles music, or that of any of the Mersey Beat groups such as The Searchers or even Gerry and the Pacemakers.

Wayne played on the right of midfield. The Anfield crowd were on his case immediately the game kicked off. They were targeting him with the usual abuse, and some of it concerned Laura Simpson. They were also trying out a new song about 'Fathead Sam and his band of freaks'. The visceral tension palpably increased every time Wayne was on the ball. Sometimes Ferguson had left him out of the adrenalin-rushed clashes with Liverpool because he feared that the occasion might have overwhelmed and unnerved him. The problem was that Wayne's whole life can be viewed as an endless search for an adrenalin hit.

There was another layer of tension to be dissipated because of the rivalry between Sam and Jürgen Klopp, relating back to the time when the former had been in charge of Sunderland. It concerned a comment Allardyce had made about Klopp being a 'soft German' after a tackle by one of the hard-nut Sunderland defenders on the sublime Coutinho. The challenge had outraged Klopp.

Such namby-pamby nonsense was not an issue to be fretted about in Sam's time as a gargantuan centre-half for Bolton. (I saw Allardyce play for them and even Rhino would have swerved him.) In the PC world we live in (and I am not talking laptops here), it caused a stir. Sam had guided Sunderland to safety two years previously, after taking charge when they were second from the bottom. When he left David Moyes took over and some say he took them down.

Liverpool dominated the game but Allardyce had masterminded a disciplined, well-organised performance. Three minutes from half-time Liverpool went ahead with a fine goal from the accomplished Mohamed Salah after an assist by Joe Gomez. It was his nineteenth goal of the season and it wasn't even Christmas. The ex-Chelsea winger, discarded by Mourinho for his aristo indulgences, hit a left-footed shot from the right side of the penalty area.

Sam changed things around in the break, sending on Schneiderlin and Lennon for Niasse and Davies. This freed things up for Wayne to play further forward and centrally. This suited him better; he was less static and consequently, Everton looked far livelier.

Thirteen minutes from the end Dominic Calvert-Lewin was judged to have been pushed by Dejan Lovren, who was yellow-carded. It was a delicious, slide-rule pass from Wayne that had released him into the box. The same move had almost caught out Liverpool early in the second half but the nervy Calvert-Lewin was faced with two possible courses of action: passing to Sigurdsson or shooting, but was caught in two minds.

The penalty kick was Wayne at his coolest; it was only the second Everton penalty to be awarded at Anfield since 1937 and could not be wasted. An almost sinister iciness took him over, for now he was only concerned with one thing: putting the ball into the back of the Liverpool net. Totally self-absorbed, he had this amazing ability to put absolutely everything out of his mind. He waited calmly for Simon Mignolet to commit himself, then chipped it straight down the middle.

In subsequent interviews he told *Match of the Day* that the Liverpool keeper had saved a couple of his previous penalties from him and had decided to go that route. Talking to Alan Brazil in the talkSPORT interview, he described it as follows, saying, 'There was a lot of pressure – no one else was taking it. From my angle it was a clear penalty. I was banking on the goalkeeper diving.'

Two minutes after his successful penalty conversion Wayne was replaced by Phil Jagielka, who was fit again after missing the win over Huddersfield. Sam wanted to safeguard the precious point, and the stats revealed that Liverpool had 72 per cent possession and twelve corners compared to Everton's solitary one. Wayne's penalty had enabled Everton to draw the 229th Merseyside derby though, and another item on his bucket list was ticked off.

The following Wednesday, Everton went to St James Park for a midweek Premier fixture against Rafael Benítez's Newcastle United. The Geordies had lost six in seven winless games and were desperate for points. Wayne added to their misery by scoring the only goal of the game from one of their few chances, and it was a game like the fourth coffee on a January morning. Rooney was no longer a tornado but a bolt of lightning that could strike at any time. And strike he did, after twenty-seven minutes with a simple goal. Aaron Lennon, the smallest player on the pitch, rose to out-jump the Newcastle defence and direct a header to their goalkeeper, Karl Darlow. It contained no real power, but the unfortunate sausage-fingered custodian spilled the ball and Wayne slid in at the far post to score from point-blank range.

It may have looked simple – a standard poke of the boot – but the difficult bit was anticipating the action and being in the right spot. That night in Newcastle, Wayne demonstrated all the essential qualities of why he was such a great, record-breaking striker: quick reflexes, perfect timing, a sense of anticipation and being always superbly alert to any opportunity. Rooney could score goals which to most players were not there. He did not appear to move with any real speed. The crucial thing was that he moved first; he put it away before any of the Newcastle players could get to him. In these games Wayne had recaptured the verve of his early post-millennial imperial phase, albeit refocused through the lens of a player of thirty-two, with dwindling physical powers.

Henry, Shearer and Wayne all emerged as the great opportunists of the Premier era because they displayed that single-mindedness in the most claustrophobic of situations. Today we have the neurotic perfectionists Griezmann, Kane, Agüero and Sanchez. Alexis opened his Manchester United account following his move from Arsenal with a simple tap-in against Huddersfield after his penalty kick had been saved. It is impossible for a young player to be taught the quality of anticipation, which is instinctive amongst the great goal-scorers of their generation.

Newcastle had no luck in the Everton game. Seconds

before Rooney's match-winner, they had struck the post with a rasping shot from Ritchie. The upright was still wobbling with the ferocity of the drive when Everton broke away to score. Just before half-time Mikel Merino's long-range effort crashed against the other post. Everton's defence held firm in the second half as their midfield controlled the tempo of the game. Thirteen minutes from time Wayne left the field to be replaced by the mercurial Tom Davies.

In his talkSPORT interview with Alan Brazil, Wayne extolled the virtues of his new coach: 'He has made us hard to beat, has you organised, wants you to play football. Nowadays a lot of science goes into making you better. We have calculated sessions, balance of rest days.'

Alan Brazil asked him where he was happiest playing. Wayne replied that he had played in the traditional Number 10 role against Newcastle after dropping deeper for the Huddersfield and Hammers games.

So Everton were unbeaten under Allardyce with three wins out of four and a resurgent Wayne back amongst the goals. So far that season he had notched nine goals out of twenty-four shots and had a conversion rate of 38 per cent, which was easily the best ratio of the top strikers. Harry Kane had twelve Premier goals but had put in exactly one hundred shots.

Next up were Swansea on a Monday night fixture at Goodison. Everton were up to tenth in the table but Swansea were rock-bottom and had been beaten seven times in their last nine games. Sam was warning against complacency. He made the point that the team was 'running on empty' after their recent busy run of games. The match was a game of penalties, both of them taken by Wayne. Swansea had taken a surprise lead through Leroy Fer after thirty-five minutes on another freezing, foggy winter's night.

A corner from Tom Carroll caused confusion and careless marking by the former Swansea captain. Williams allowed the Dutch midfielder, Fer, to jab home from close range. Williams's lack of concentration was costing Everton dear, what with his sloppy defending and cockamamie positioning. Williams was another hugely questionable purchase during the Koeman era.

In first-half injury time Everton were awarded a penalty when Roque Mesa bundled over Aaron Lennon. The winger was in excellent form, having nearly scored in the opening minutes. This was following a fine run, ending with a shot just past the post. It made Allardyce's decision a few weeks later, to move him out of the club to Burnley, surprising. Aaron had done remarkably well to come back to the Premier after experiencing a mental health problem.

Up stepped Wayne to take the kick but Fabiański flew across his goal to make a wonderful save. The ex-Arsenal keeper was one of the most underrated goalkeepers in the Premier and had guessed correctly. There's no luck when you are down at the bottom though, and the ball span out and Calvert-Lewin followed up to slot home the rebound. It was the second penalty Wayne had missed out of the last three he had taken. (Out of the trio Rooney would have been pleased that he netted the Anfield kick.) It had worked out well for Everton though, as goals had resulted from the rebounds. After the match he was asked by the *Metro* if he was contemplating letting someone else take over this duty. His answer was, 'I am a confident person and if you notice the two I have missed we've scored, so I put top spin on it and I know that we will get the rebound. I am not giving them up!'

Top spin was another facet of Wayne's game that hardly received any attention. To bend the ball to the left with his right foot, he span it in an anti-clockwise direction. This was done by making contact with the ball with the part of his foot between the hub of his big toe and the side of his foot. He practised this art for hours at the Gems when he was young, standing at an angle and bending the ball round the right-hand goalpost using his right foot. The constant practice helped him begin to control the amount of spin he could put on the ball. Sometimes the caretaker of the building would even leave the floodlights on especially, so that the young fellow in the Everton shirt could stay and practise. The more spin he imparted on the ball, the more vicious the bend or the boomerang. His hat-trick goal against West Ham is a great example of this.

The second half against Swansea was grim, as the Welsh team dug in to preserve their point. They had lost Wilfried Bony to injury early in the game and he was replaced by the young striker Tammy Abraham, who was on loan from Chelsea. Tammy had played in the same England Under-21 side as Calvert-Lewin. They were a generation of young players who were highly regarded, particularly abroad. Wayne set the second goal up for Gylfi Sigurdsson to put

PURPLE WAYNE

Everton ahead. The rolled pass found the former Swansea star, who drifted outside before firing home from thirty yards. It needed something special to beat Fabiański, but he was left helpless as the ball curled past him.

The match was sealed seventeen minutes from time when Wayne scored from the spot, this time getting the better of the Swansea goalie. There was an element of luck about the penalty, which had been awarded because of a Swansea's defender challenge on Jonjoe Kenny. TV replays indicated that the challenge was outside of the box. Had the VR technology been available that night then Wayne would have been denied his sixth goal in four matches. It is interesting to note that the three penalties he had so far converted had all been for physical challenges.

Them was the breaks for Swansea, who dispensed with the services of their boss, Paul Clement, shortly afterwards. It was all sunshine and roses for Sam Allardyce at that point, since he had taken charge and turned Everton's season around. He told the *Metro*: 'You have to have a big personality to walk into a football club and say to the players, "Look, lads, listen to me. This is what you need to do, this is how you get out of the position you are in." It's not rocket science, it's simplifying.'

But things were to change again in the coming weeks.

CHAPTER 18

THE OTHER FERGIE

'You can't burn out if you're not on fire.'
JOHNNY DEPP, ON JIM MORRISON,
IN *WHEN YOU'RE STRANGE: A FILM ABOUT THE DOORS*

Let us now discuss Wayne's relationship with Duncan Ferguson, the only player of recent times to match Rooney in terms of symbolising what being an Evertonian meant.

Duncan Cowan Ferguson, fourteen years older then him, was Wayne's childhood hero, the reason he persevered so hard at being a footballer and part of the sub-culture of Everton Football Club.

Wayne loved boxing. The Rooney family were keen fighters, and his father boxed as a lightweight for Liverpool. Wayne senior drank in bars with Irish flags and fading photographs of prizefighters on the wall. His son Wayne started boxing at around the time he first commenced training at Everton as a young whippersnapper. His uncle ran a boys' boxing club at the Croxteth Sports Centre and Wayne was a regular, indulging in sparring, low-key fisticuffs and road training. The 'Rocky' wannabe showed plenty of aggression and carried a wicked left hand. Plans for a first fight were shelved when he started experiencing back pains and also Everton told him to quit the noble art.

Rocky Marciano, the undefeated heavyweight champion, used to say that when, as a kid, he first knocked out a man in the gymnasium it was like discovering he could sing opera. When Wayne Rooney first discovered he could play football at the highest level it was like discovering he could KO opponents like Tyson at the height of his pomp.

Mike Tyson was his favourite boxer, a fighter of extraordinary power and terrifying aggression. Too young to remember Ali, Iron Mike's bewildering hand speed and ferocious punching power captured Wayne's imagination. Tyson's turbulent personality and frequent clashes with authority made a lasting impression on him. Like Duncan Ferguson, often shadowed by notoriety, Tyson served hard time. At around the time Ferguson was released from jail, Tyson had completed his three-year sentence in a facility in Indiana for rape.

Perhaps Wayne had seen Robert De Niro's Academy Award-winning performance as Jake LaMotta in Martin Scorsese's film *Raging Bull*. LaMotta also had a troubled personal life. Born on the Lower East Side of New York City to ethnically Italian parents, he achieved his success in spite of a difficult childhood. His father forced the youngster to fight other boys to entertain neighbourhood adults. The money thrown into the ring at the end of the contests was collected by his father to help pay the rent. Jake grew up to be world middleweight champion in a golden era for boxing. Famous for the vicious beatings he gave to his opponents and his ability to withstand brutal punishment, he was nicknamed 'The Raging Bull'. He ended up in prison and lost the fortune he made from boxing in what was essentially a Jacobean tragedy.

That sobriquet would have been perfect for Wayne, for he was like a bull when he was young. So powerful and belligerent, yet beneath the bravado there was, one could sense, a tension in Rooney. Men like Colin Harvey talked of him with a kind of reverence.

Both men were an immense part of the tradition of Everton Football Club. This tale of Wayne's explosive arrival as a major star is a familiar one, and timing had a great deal to do with it. Future social historians, students of Everton Football Club and psychologists will have a field day with their bonding.

Duncan Ferguson was a legendary figure during Wayne's youth. He was the hardest, most controversial player of his generation and the first professional footballer to go to prison for an offence that was committed on the pitch. Ferguson spent a tempestuous decade at Everton punctuated by an unhappy spell at Newcastle United.

The incident that was to dominate Ferguson's career occurred in April 1994 when he was playing for Glasgow

Rangers and clashed with a Raith Rovers full-back, John 'Jock' McStay. The game was played at Ibrox in front of 42,545 fans and Rangers ended up winning 4–0, with Ferguson scoring the third. It was his first goal for Rangers in fourteen appearances since joining them from Dundee United. The deal, at that time a British transfer record of £4 million, made him the country's most expensive player. Ibrox was where the money grew back then. Trevor Stephen, Terry Butcher, Gazza and Ray Wilkins had all ended up at Ibrox in big money deals. After the players jostled for the ball the referee blew for a foul by Ferguson. Duncan then turned to the full-back and head-butted McStay. The player went down clutching his face, as if Tyson had clipped him. After receiving treatment, the game was restarted. Ferguson was not even booked at the time.

Ferguson was signed by Everton from Rangers initially on a loan deal of three months in October 1994. The package included Ian Durrant, who joined for a month. Scotland midfielder Durrant was another brilliant prospect whose career was wrecked by a knee injury. This was sustained in a clash with the Aberdeen player Neil Simpson and resulted in Ian tearing the cruciate ligaments in his right knee. This put him out of football for almost three seasons. The incident is still regarded as a problem between the two sides nearly thirty years later. Durrant later sued Simpson for damages and the case was settled out of court. At Everton he only played five games but poignant flashes of the player that he could have been were still apparent.

THE OTHER FERGIE

The Toffees were precariously placed near the bottom of the Premier and the acquisition of Ferguson smacked of desperation, if not panic. Although still in his early twenties, he was seen as a flop, having scored just two League goals in fifteen months, and he made just twenty-three appearances for Rangers: indeed a poor contribution for £4 million. What's more he carried more baggage around with him than Elton John on a Louis Vuitton-sponsored world tour.

The main feature of his play was his ultra-aggressive and highly competitive attitude. Duncan had developed a reputation of being a menace on the field, with his constant stalking and brawling, in the same manner Iron Mike and the 'Raging Bull' LaMotta character pummelled their opponents in the ring. A parallel could be drawn to the recent successful Chelsea teams that included the battering ram centre forwards Drogba and Costa, who would slug it out with even the toughest defences.

In his early days at Everton Wayne must have identified strongly with Duncan in terms of the great expectations placed on his massive shoulders and his disciplinary problems. Both men were to learn by bitter experience about the hypocrisy of fame. Wayne was an aggressive player, another enfant terrible, but alongside Ferguson he was serene and uncomplicated. Duncan was furious at the Scottish authorities: he had a twelve-match ban hanging over him, at that time an unprecedented suspension in British football. More tellingly, he had been charged by Strathclyde Police. Ferguson's legal team protested that the Scottish Football Association's ban prejudiced his forthcoming court trial. At the start of their careers both Ferguson and Rooney were portrayed as being tough bruisers from poor council estates, both arrogant and irritable. Wayne quickly learnt that the only way to reach the very top was to create an army of admirers of his skill. More importantly, those admirers had to include the Establishment and the media. It seems apparent that the vituperative authorities wanted to make an example of Ferguson because of his contempt for them and his refusal to submit to their yoke. Ferguson's reputation was as demanding as a crack addiction, and he was the perfect scapegoat.

Just as Rooney's legend was born with his goal against Arsenal, then Ferguson's performance against Liverpool in his maiden Mersey derby won the crowd for him. A crowd he never lost to this day. In his seventh game in an Everton shirt, Duncan was playing in the Mersey derby. Everton had won this just once in their first sixteen games. Liverpool were riding high, handily placed fourth. It was Joe Royle's first game in charge, and he was a true Evertonian, a man who knew a thing or two about centre-forward play; a revered Number 9 who had scored one hundred goals in 275 games.

Duncan headed the first goal, soaring above Liverpool keeper David James and Neil 'Razor' Ruddock to thump home Andy Hinchcliffe's precise corner. Ruddock had turned a subdued Ferguson into the Incredible Hulk when he had kicked him in the backside a few minutes before. Razor Ruddock would not have liked him when he was angry.

The Scottish striker celebrated by doing a knee skid in

front of the Gwladys Street End, which was also in line with an advert for Carling lager. Just a few hours before the derby game he had been breathalysed for crashing his car into a bus garage. You couldn't make it up.

If you watch players such as Mesut Özil for Arsenal take corners, it looks like he is trying to individually pick a player out. Hinchliffe did not do that, even though it looks as if he did, because Ferguson arrived on the end of it. Hinchcliffe used to attack three areas: the far post, the middle and the near post. He would put the ball along a trajectory. It was not rocket science, as Big Sam says.

Ferguson set the second goal up for Paul Rideout with a clever pass across the box and Everton won a famous victory 2–0. The marauder that was Ferguson did not play football that day, he inflicted it on the Liverpool rearguard. Neville Southall played in goal for Everton in that match and heaped praise on Ferguson in an interview for the book *Faith of Our Families: Everton FC, an Oral History*: 'He had been a bit lost on the pitch in his first weeks at the club, but when we faced our neighbours in Joe's first game he went to war. Duncan should have been – and I have said this on numerous occasions – the best player in the world. But he just wasn't motivated enough to do that.'

As a player who had the motivation, Wayne Rooney was transfixed when he watched the game with his father, Ferguson being the epicentre of a new world. Soon a poster would appear on his bedroom wall of Duncan in his Everton shirt powering home that fantastic header. Perhaps 'Duncan the player' best reflected 'Everton the team' at that point in time: he was combative, attritional and cynical. A tall, strong, aggressive centre-forward had always been a tradition at Goodison since the dawn of time, ranging from Dixie Dean to Graham Sharp. We have seen how Koeman's failure to sign such a player after Lukaku departed cost him his job. Chelsea never looked the same team once Costa had been sold to Atletico Madrid after falling out with his coach Conte.

Duncan Ferguson was born in Bannockburn, ironically the scene of a famous victory in the fourteenth century wars of Scottish Independence. It was here that Robert the Bruce defeated King Edward II. A few miles up the road at Stirling Castle there is a monument commemorating William Wallace, who led the Scottish rebellion against Edward I. You may know him better as 'Braveheart' in the melodramatic movie of that name starring Mel Gibson. Cardboard cut-outs of the 'Braveheart' character are still taken to Internationals by members of the Tartan Army.

Ferguson lived on a council estate known as 'Legoland', referred to as such because the houses looked like pieces of Lego. It was a typical working-class area, like the kind of settings described in a William McIlvanney crime novel.

Signed by Dundee United as a schoolboy he made rapid progress and soon gatecrashed the Scotland team. Ferguson only played for twelve minutes in the Euro 1992 competition, coming on against Holland. Dennis Bergkamp had scored the only goal of the game. The Dutch team was packed with bona fide greats, including Ruud Gullit (who was to sign him for Newcastle in November 1998 when he was briefly manager), Marco van Basten, Frank Rijkaard and a certain Ronald Koeman.

Ferguson was a moody player, and his enthusiasm seemed to fluctuate depending on his mood. The difference between the two men was that Wayne, as we have seen throughout this book, just loved football. Whether it was kicking a ball against a brick wall or past a Premier goalkeeper it didn't matter, it was playing the game that he enjoyed. We have seen him come home after match-winning performances for Everton and then join his mates out in the street for a kick-about. Ferguson's manager at Dundee United, the crotchety Jim McLean, was on record as saying that if his club had paid Duncan for staying at home he would not have bothered turning up to play football.

When Ferguson joined Rangers he had to displace Mark Hateley, the ex AC Milan and England centre-forward. This proved difficult, as the experienced striker found a rich vein of form, and it was hard to break into an established, successful side. When Wayne broke into the Everton team and later, following his transfer the Manchester United set-up, he went in automatically. Nobody challenged him and there was little resentment amongst his new teammates.

After the Mersey Derby 'Dunc-mania' took over the biggest phenomenon since 'Beatle-mania' in the city of Liverpool. I do not know if Wayne sported a 'Big Dunc' tee-shirt. The crowd used to get in early before kick-off to watch the big man do keepie-ups. At Christmas 1994 he signed a permanent deal with Everton and scored seven goals over the coming months. The most memorable one was a replica of the goal he scored against Liverpool, except that this time it was against Manchester United. Hinchcliffe curled over a corner and Duncan jumped above Roy Keane to head home the only goal of the game. This led to the wild celebrations when he tore off his Number-9 shirt and, glistening with testosterone, twirled it above his head. This sparked a warning letter from the English FA, who deemed these antics to be 'a display of triumphalism and excessive'.

An interesting stat was that in his first spell at the club he scored fifteen headers out of his first twenty-five goals Yet after his return to Everton from Newcastle not one of his first seventeen goals were with his head.

A hamstring injury ruled him out for the rest of the season except for one more substitute appearance. That was another big one, when he came on after fifty-one minutes in the FA Cup final to replace the match-winner Paul Rideout. To say he put himself about would be an understatement, winning headers and appearing in the centre of the action. After the match he celebrated by wearing a comedy clown's blue nose on the lap of honour and a kilt of the Ferguson tartan at the celebration dinner.

After three adjournments Duncan became the first footballer to serve a jail term for an on-the-pitch assault, for which he was sentenced to three months in prison. Andy Hinchcliffe was shocked by the verdict and said in the book *Faith of Our Families: Everton FC, an Oral History*: 'Whatever happens on a football field, we did not expect them to lead to custodial sentences. And you always think that it is not going to happen to one of our guys.

We know he could be fairly volatile and aggressive, but he is lovely. Obviously, we had seen the incident but we thought it would not happen.'

Sheriff Eccles, who sentenced Duncan, was unmoved by a letter written by Everton management, detailing their striker's time spent coaching youngsters on Merseyside, plus his frequent visits to children's hospitals. The Lancashire Probation Service had recommended community service rather than prison, but this advice went unheeded. Wayne was following the trial closely and years later, when doing his court-ordered community service, he spoke of its benefits to society. Over the years Rooney had been a frequent visitor to the children's hospice where his sister-in-law Rosie had died in 2013.

Ferguson served his time in Barlinnie, Scotland's toughest jail, a hard man amongst hard men and deranged gangland villains. It seemed almost ironic that Celtic Park was the next building on the Scottish skyline. The Number 9 on the back of Duncan's Everton shirt was now replaced by Number 12718 on a red jumper, because the Everton-blue jumpers were worn by prisoners on remand. That number still relates to Duncan, as it would appear that they are not re-allocated. In another twist of fate, the prison governor had been at Ibrox to watch Rangers take on Raith Rovers on that fateful day.

When Ferguson was incarcerated, Wayne, then aged about nine, had written to him twice. Copies of the correspondence would be highly collectable today. In the letters, Wayne wrote that his idol should not be in prison and that he and his little chums were very keen for Duncan to return to Goodison and play for the Toffees. Duncan had received sackfuls of mail from his legion of fans and spent a great deal of his time replying to them personally. Wayne was made up when he received a letter back from Duncan, thanking him for his support.

The first time Wayne had met Duncan Ferguson was at Bellefield. It was when the three Rooney brothers were together at the Academy. Someone had come up with the idea of a photographic session, and Wayne admitted that Ferguson did not know who the little boys were and that he had no recollection of meeting them before. Wayne's lasting memory of the meeting was how big Ferguson was, a similar experience to the way he felt when he was mascot for the Liverpool game and met Dave Watson.

When Wayne made the first team and started training with the big names he came into daily contact with Ferguson and they hit it off right away. On his first day with the team Ferguson had come over specially to wish him well. Usually a reserved, world-weary personality, Duncan always had time for the younger players and showed a friendlier side of his nature to them. Wayne always maintained that the tartan terror had a very young outlook on life and in a way found it easier to communicate with the youngsters.

On a pre-season tour of Austria, Wayne had a wrestling match with him following a friendly dispute over a computer golf game. They both shared a love for gaming and on away trips Wayne would spend time in his company, battling away with the latest graphics in straight-up button bashing.

Ferguson considered himself to be not only a great player but a world-class games specialist.

In that difficult second season when Wayne's relationship with David Moyes started to unravel, the Everton manager warned him to stay away from Ferguson. The Everton boss's view was that the ex-Rangers striker was a bad influence on him. But Ferguson was now a mentor to Rooney, something that was obvious to everyone in the club.

Wayne ridiculed this warning and repeated it in the dressing room in front of the rest of the team. Ferguson scoffed at this, with his trademark corrosive wit to the fore, but like Wayne he was also having problems with the manager. Ferguson thought Moyes was trying to move him out of Goodison to reduce the wage bill, by telling him he had no future in the club.

Kevin Kilbane, who joined Everton in 2003, the year after Rooney made his first team debut, described Ferguson becoming a father figure for Wayne. The young striker trusted Ferguson and liked him because he never wanted anything back from him. At that time Wayne was the hottest property in the game and everyone he came in contact with wanted a piece of him, sometimes they wanted more like a chunk. There were hangers-on, basking in his reflected glory, hustlers and lowlifes trying to make money out of him. Lesser talents trying to go further than they could on their own by getting a tow from Wayne's talent.

Ferguson only made eight appearances in Rooney's first season, all of them from the bench. By now the Scotsman's career was in decline, he was, frustrated by his lack of success, disappointed at the differences with management, and ruined by injuries and loss of form. You could liken him to a burning Zero fighter plane falling from the sky. Wayne was muscling onto his Goodison turf, the new kid on the block.

The well of sympathy and pity for Ferguson, from which he had drunk long and hard, was slowly running dry with some Evertonians. His injuries were causing a lack of mobility and his high wages were becoming a sticking point with many of them.

The parallels with Andy Carroll became more apparent. Whilst Carroll was not in Ferguson's class as a player, the physicality of both players is remarkable. There has always been a demand for that type of striker willing to take and give knocks. The problem was that their shelf life was short and the burnout factor was high.

The blue shirts with the name of 'Rooney' emblazoned on the back were now outselling the versions with Ferguson's name on them. It must have been hard for Ferguson to watch things change around him, and must have engendered a growing sadness. Always the hard man, he knew that it was harder to stay at the top than to reach it, mainly because life has no justice. It must be worse nowadays, with the young players frazzled and blinded by crazy money and instant power.

The only recorded incident between the two men was when the uber-striker Rooney provided the assist for Ferguson to score his first ever goal at Hampden Park: a lifetime's ambition for Ferguson, which had eluded him for all of his career. Admittedly the goal Wayne laid on was against Queens Park in a pre-season friendly, but it was still Hampden after all. This was in July 2002 in a match that Everton won 6–0. Legend has it that the unruffled Ferguson did not acknowledge Wayne's part in it.

Their friendship endured though, and it never approached a sell-by date. At the time of writing they are still working together, since both of them are back at Goodison.

CHAPTER 19

LOOK WHAT YOU COULD HAVE WON

'For sure Wayne Rooney is one of the best players for Everton. It was a great buy. He is showing he is a fantastic player. I think he is a player who plays with his soul.'

ANTONIO CONTE

DECEMBER 2017

The legendary, late darts gameshow host Jim Bowen had a great catchphrase which was, 'Look what you could have won.'

This was traditionally said to a losing contestant on his wonderful *Bullseye* TV show. The prizes were always bizarre, with no relevance to the socio-economic group of the contestants. For example, if you were a binman living in Rotherham, what would you be doing with a speedboat? Jim used to wrap up the show by saying: 'All you've got is your bus fare home.'

In similar vein, Everton must have been thinking about what they could have won. Sadly, the Europa League and the Carabao Cup had already gone for the season.

Wayne's performances were coming under increasing scrutiny again as the press went into overdrive about him scoring six goals in his last five games. In all he had scored ten Premier goals in sixteen games, and it was the fastest he had reached that target in five years.

Under Koeman, Everton had played a short passing game from the back, which did not work. They were losing the ball in dangerous areas and being punished for it. When Wayne did receive the ball, it was in a crowded area. There were no out balls to play or options. Sam Allardyce changed it around by going long, and since he had taken over the average attempted passes at Everton had dropped from 430 under Koeman to 359. The game plan was to use the pace of Calvert-Lewin to make space for Wayne, with Sigurdsson backing up.

The next game was a lunchtime Saturday home match against Chelsea and it was the third time they had met the champions in a few months. Chelsea captain Gary Cahill was looking forward to renewing his acquaintance with Rooney, which had been formed when they were on England duty together. He told *The Sun*: 'I get on really well with him, he oozes class in terms of ability, in terms of experience, winning trophies, his pedigree in the game. Sometimes you see him get criticism but he can just roll out his CV and what he has done in the game is incredible.'

Cahill did not get to renew his acquaintance with Wayne

because Rooney missed the game due to catching a virus. A few days before his illness struck he was photographed in the press donating a quarter of a million pounds to the Claire House Children's Hospice on behalf of his Wayne Rooney Foundation.

Wayne did not miss much of a game, as it finished 0–0, on a characteristically foggy, rainy day. Chelsea dominated, having 68 per cent possession and peppering the Everton goal with twenty-five shots in several onslaughts (Everton had a total of five shots). For all their dominance, Chelsea did not create as many chances as Antonio Conte would have hoped for. Throughout the season he had suggested that Chelsea were struggling to cope with their schedule yet he continued to keep his players on a strict training routine.

Eden Hazard, leading the line in place of the suspended Álvaro Morata, was a constant threat with his driving runs. The only real chance Everton had in the game was just before half-time, when Dominic Calvert-Lewin selfishly tried to dribble through a pack of defenders rather than pass to the unmarked Gylfi Sigurdsson. As the game died on its feet Chelsea almost stole it when the hapless Ashley Williams glanced a cross against his own bar. Pickford, arms akimbo, could only watch on helplessly.

Everton defended in increasing depth, just leaving Sandro Ramirez up front and ground out a valuable point. By going back to basics Sam had lifted them up the table, but a game like this made many Everton fans uncomfortable. Allardyce seemed too brash and full of himself for some Evertonians, who preferred their managers to be humble and understated.

When Moyes joined Everton as a young manager from Preston North End, he had brought in new ideas to the club and was a breath of fresh air. Walter Smith, whom he had replaced, was seen as old school. It was Moyes who had coined 'the people's club of Merseyside' phrase. A young coach with pedigree, Champions League credentials, or at least aspirations, was top of most fans' wish list.

Then it was Christmas, and the presenters on TV were screaming about how terrible it would be if you didn't get your Christmas shopping done in time. It would be terrible anyway: it always is. Big Sam came over like the benevolent character George Bailey in the feel-good Christmas film favourite *It's a Wonderful Life* by giving the players Christmas Day off. The Everton boss claimed that in his twenty years of management he had never brought his players in for training on that day. This was because when he was a player he loathed having to come in over Yuletide. Charles Dickens would have loved his ideas.

In his talkSPORT interview, Wayne told Alan Brazil that he spent Christmas morning at home with his kids and after the traditional dinner he would have a rest in the evening. Brazil asked him his views on a winter break, which was being mooted again. Wayne said that he could see both sides of the matter but would not bank on a break coming anytime soon.

At least he was with his family as he tried to weather the storm of the early autumn. Shortly before Christmas, Coleen made a statement on Facebook, saying that she was investing in her marriage and declaring her love for Wayne.

LOOK WHAT YOU COULD HAVE WON

> Do I love Wayne? Yes, I do. If I didn't I would not
> be trying to make it work. I am not going to list his
> good qualities, I don't think he deserves it, but he is
> a brilliant dad.
>
> I know I would be fine on my own with just me
> and the children but I don't want to live like that.
> I want to try and continue our marriage and live as
> a family.

Her moving statement displayed her strength of character.
I have never seen an interview or photograph of this young
woman that did not radiate her genuine goodness. Rooney
is a lucky man to have her in his life, a rock against the
forces that have destroyed cleverer and even more talented
individuals. Well, readers, some footballers' wives could
have developed skin cancer from too much basking in their
husbands' reflected glory, but not her.

Tony Hancock was a comedian whose life had the
potential of a Greek tragedy. Committing suicide after being
addicted to drink was a sad end to his once brilliant career.
He observed that resilience was a prerequisite to survive in
the cut-throat world of showbiz. The same thing applies to
footballers and, by extension, footballers' wives. Look up
resilience in the dictionary and you will see a picture of the
Rooneys from Croxteth.

The only thing that put a dampener on Wayne's Crimbo
was that the virus continued to lay him low and he was
confined to bed for four days with a fever. As a result, he
missed the Boxing Day trip to West Bromwich Albion,

who were crashing down the League like an old lift. They had not won in seventeen League games and never looked like breaking the record that day. A poor game played in persistent rain threw up a predictable 0–0 draw, the second consecutive match Everton had been in a goal-free zone. They played at an ever-increasing, ever-frenetic pace with plenty of strong and determined individuals but lacked the magic, the element of the unexpected, that Rooney could provide.

Wayne was back in the squad for the next match against Bournemouth away, the last match of 2017. Big Sam was interviewed in the midday BBC Soccer show by Mark Lawrenson, ex-Liverpool defender and a man of eccentric appearance, who had a strange taste in shirts and waistcoats, all of which appeared to be two sizes too small. When asked about Wayne, a self-congratulatory Sam replied that he no longer regarded him as a striker, saying, 'He had not been one for a while.'

In a form league based on the games since Sam had taken over at Everton, his team would have been in fifth position in the table. The big man cracked a smile as big as a Cheshire cat.

Allardyce kept Wayne on the bench in the first half as Everton trailed to a Ryan Fraser goal. Calvert-Lewin had played in every Everton fixture so far except the dead rubber game against Limasoll, and was suffering combat fatigue. James McCarthy, playing his first League game in almost a year, had gifted Bournemouth with their opening goal after making an atrocious back pass. Wayne replaced him at half-time and operated in midfield for the duration. Idrissa Gueye equalised on the hour after an assist by Niasse. The goal-scorer was replaced by the former Palace winger Yannick Bolasie, playing for the first time since a serious injury. It was the first time he and Rooney had played in the same side together. Wayne had a subdued forty-five minutes, floundering in midfield, still weakened by the virus. His one major contribution was a snapshot that whistled narrowly wide. A bullish Allardyce sensed victory but it was Bournemouth who stole the points in the last minute. Jonjoe Kenny was caught out too far up field and the overlapping wing-back, Smith, took full advantage to put Fraser in for the winner. Pickford may have saved the shot but it took a deflection off Keane. Wayne stared glassily into space as he trudged off the field.

Happy New Year.

The full-back positions were a problem to Everton, and Kenny's lack of experience had cost them the points at the Vitality Stadium. There were also concerns about Martina having sufficient quality for the Premier League, and the club desperately missed right-sided defender Seamus Colman, who was approaching fitness after a long absence.

For their first home fixture of 2018 Manchester United were the visitors on another cold evening on the first day at the beginning of the new year. Sam made seven changes from the team beaten at Bournemouth. Wayne made the starting line-up but two second-half goals by José Mourinho's men were enough to give United their first win in five matches and leave Sam without a win in four games.

WAYNE ROONEY

It was not a good night for Wayne against his old side, the team he had scored a record 253 goals for. Playing for Sir Alex Ferguson, reaching his seventy-sixth birthday a few days before and moving irretrievably into old age, seemed a lifetime ago. Wayne was caught in possession for the move that set the Reds up for the first goal in fifty-seven minutes. Paul Pogba, at last looking like something approaching a £90-million player, seized the ball and found Martial with a fine pass. Martial, insanely popular with the United fans, curled the ball around Pickford for his fourth strike in six games against Everton.

Amazingly, it was Everton's first New Year's Day fixture for fifteen years at Goodison. The previous one had been a 2–2 draw against Manchester City in which a young Wayne Rooney had played. The first half was dull. United were missing the injured Romelu Lukaku in what would have been his return to the club that he made his name with. Mourinho was coiled and dangerous that night, clearly ready for trouble, his eyes glittering.

Anthony Martial was playing in that role in the continued absence of the mesmerising Zlatan Ibrahimović. Wayne, with no boyishness left, was operating in midfield alongside the bright young thing who was Tom Davies. A corner was won by a deflected shot from Wayne but that was his main contribution in the first half. He was later booked for chopping down Martial. Shortly after Martial scored, Wayne was subbed and replaced by James McCarthy (a reversal of the substitution in the previous game at Bournemouth). Sam, disappointed at the Rooney error that led to the United opener, was also conscious of the fact that he just could no longer play so many games within a couple of days. Wayne looked disconsolate as both sets of fans acknowledged his contribution to them with generous applause.

Nine minutes from time, with some Evertonians already leaving for the warmth of their firesides, Jesse Lingard scored the second for United, tearing past Michael Keane to curl a shot past Pickford. United had dominated the second half with 65 per cent possession – and almost twice as many completed passes. One telling stat emerged from the match: Everton had not managed a single attempt on target. In an effort to remedy the lack of goals and the big gaping hole in their attack they had purchased Cenk Tossun from Beşiktaş for £25 million.

Cenk Tossun was a late replacement for Lukaku, the striker who had scored twenty-four goals the previous season and half that figure so far in the current term. The German-born Turkish international (who had scored eight goals in twenty-five games) had the advantage of being able to speak English which was always useful. Wayne had reached double figures by mid-December but the rigours of the season were catching up with him. Those goals were worth ten points,which he had independently won, and Everton would have been second from bottom in the Premier without them.

Then it was the big one: Liverpool away in the third round of the FA Cup. It was the first time the great Merseyside rivals had met in the competition since the 2012 semi-final. A late winner from Andy Carroll took the Reds to the final, where they had lost to Chelsea. You had to go back awhile for a Merseyside Cup win: 2006 for Liverpool and 1995 for the Toffees' win over Manchester United.

Now the clubs had different agendas and priorities. Jürgen Klopp, the Premier's most enigmatic character, was desperate to stay in the top four and have a run in the Champions League. For Allardyce the priority was survival, and the Toffees' appalling form under Koeman was still raw and he was fully aware of how any slump in form could suck them down in a relegation battle. Having said that, the FA Cup was the last chance of winning any silverware.

Wayne was desperate to bring a trophy to his beloved club before he signed off his career. The problem was that the clock was ticking for him. An ominous sign was that his current boss had a particular reputation for treating the oldest cup in English football as very much the poor relation compared to the excessive wealth of the Premier League. Betfred bookmakers were giving 11–1 for Everton to win at Anfield with Rooney, scorer of the penalty leveller a few weeks before, 4–1 to score a goal at any point in the tie.

The match was one of those Friday games shown live on BBC One, the game that always meant Wayne's favourite TV soap was rescheduled. Everton fans snapped up all their ticket allocation and filled the Anfield end, and it was debatable if any of the 8,000 were wearing a T-shirt that had been available on the club's official website. The garment had been illustrated with fans on the Anfield Kop, with a blue background and an Everton club badge. The picture for the design was taken from a Liverpool home game against Don Revie's Leeds side in 1969. The shirt was quickly withdrawn from sale, and I am not sure if any are available on eBay

The match was not the happiest for Wayne. He only lasted fifty-two minutes before he was replaced by Ademola Lookman. Wayne was furious but Sam Allardyce had taken him off before he was sent off. A few minutes earlier Rooney, already on a caution, had been involved in a scuffle with Liverpool's Emre Can and was lucky not to receive a second yellow card. The German midfielder had unceremoniously robbed Wayne of the ball by the touchline and he had tried to retrieve in typical fashion.

Everton trailed to a first-half penalty from James Milner awarded by referee Bobby Madley after Mason Holgate had grabbed hold of midfielder Adam Lallana. The Liverpool player, now sporting a strange seventies prog-rock band haircut, went to ground and Milner, one of Rooney's class of 92, slotted home. Mason Holgate, the former Barnsley prodigy, was a developing young talent but his inexperience was shown up in sticky games like this. He had been compared to John Stones because the Manchester City and England defender had taken the same path from South Yorkshire to Merseyside.

A grim-looking Peter Reid was in the studio summarising, and made the point that Everton looked better when Rooney went off. It seemed a strange thing to say, although the subs had rejuvenated Everton. There was always the possibility that England's greatest goal-scorer may have been a catalyst for victory.

Out of the blue, with just over twenty minutes left, Everton equalised after a brilliant move. Wayne's genius third goal against West Ham was without doubt the club's best goal of the season but the equaliser scored by Gylfi Sigurdsson was the best worked. Bolasie was slowly feeling his way back to form after his terrible knee injury sent the young matador Lookman skimming through. The Everton sub, destined for the Bundesliga, calmly picked out the supporting Jagielka. The defender could have shot from a good position but instead impeccably rolled the ball to Sigurdsson, who scored with a wonderful low drive. Karius, in the Liverpool goal, had no chance as the ball flew into the net. Lookman's part in the goal should not be underrated. It seemed extraordinary that Allardyce wanted him to go out on loan to the anonymity of a Championship side rather than learn his trade in Germany.

The Everton fans behind the goal went wild, and a replay looked within their capabilities. Near the end Dominic Calvert-Lewin, who had run himself into the ground, was replaced by Niasse to shore up the midfield. The camera panned to Big Sam blatantly interrogating the legend that was Duncan Ferguson, and the colossus looked relaxed. With six minutes left Virgil van Dijk headed the winner for Liverpool from a corner: the oldest trick of all. Pickford was at fault, failing to come for a ball that he should have made his own. The former Sunderland player had a poor match, diving far too early for the penalty. Joey Barton was not convinced of his abilities and doubted that he had the qualities to become England's number-one choice.

LOOK WHAT YOU COULD HAVE WON

The ex-Southampton player had only just joined Liverpool in a world record transfer fee of £75 million for a defender. The twenty-six-year-old Dutch International had agreed personal terms in the region of £180,000 a week. A portion of his fee had been repaid by that goal.

So, Everton slipped out of the Cup, no Wembley for them. Wayne, with a hood over his head, walked slowly away into the night. Look what you could have won: the FA Cup.

But he did not need his bus fare home.

CHAPTER 20

LITTLE BOY BLUE

'Players' attitudes have changed because
of money. Getting vast amounts takes away the
hunger, that little edge.'
ALAN BALL, ENGLAND WORLD CUP WINNER

SPRING 2003

A gangster who was jailed for the murder of Rhys Jones, an eleven-year-old Everton fan, was paroled in February 2018. Rhys was killed as he walked home from football practice in Croxteth, hit by a bullet fired by a member of a criminal gang known as the Croxteth Crew in 2007. The story of his death was dramatised in a TV drama called *Little Boy Blue*. The show featured Stephen Graham, a Liverpool fan famous for his part in another seminal TV show called *This is England*, directed by Shane Meadows. Rhys was a promising youngster who had aspirations of playing for Everton.

The point is that if things had been different Wayne Rooney could have been exposed to incidents like this if he had not had football to occupy his time. 'Crocky', as Croxteth was known, was rough and scary, and the only promising option that a young boy living within its confines could envision was joining a gang. Perhaps there was something in the water. Reader, just consider the improbability of a young man rising out of Wayne's deprived background to achieve all that he did in football.

Fresh from his scene-stealing triumphs in an England shirt, Wayne returned to the Everton side. The next goal he scored was against Arsenal at Highbury at the end of March 2003. It was the first time that Wayne had started an away fixture in the Premier League and he did well to hold his own in a tense first half. Arsenal were anxious to exact revenge for their defeat at Goodison, which had cost them their unbeaten record. The Arsenal centre-back, Pascal Cygan, headed them in front after eight minutes from Thierry Henry's beautifully flighted, inswinging corner. Richard Wright, back at his old club, mis-timed the flight of the ball and Cygan arched his back to score his first goal for the club.

Though he had a quiet first half Wayne nearly conjured an equaliser for the Toffees when he galloped down the right and crossed for Mark Pembridge to turn past the post. Early in the second half, Wayne set up his pal Kevin Campbell for a chance, but the ex-Arsenal striker hit the side netting when he'd been well placed.

Taking matters into his own hands, Wayne scored a

delightful equaliser, almost in the same class as his winner against the same team. Campbell fed Wayne; he ran straight into the heart of the Arsenal defence as Cygan back-pedalled. As he neared goal the Everton striker dispatched a low shot through Cygan's legs and past the onrushing Arsenal goalkeeper Stuart Taylor. It was a great individual goal scored with aplomb. David Moyes went for a point: he was trying to secure a UEFA Cup place.

Arsenal had their own agenda though, which was trying to catch the eventual winners – Manchester United. They clinched the points when Patrick Viera shot the winner after some tomfoolery in the Everton rearguard. Rhino protested that he should have won a free kick when he clashed with the imperious Dennis Bergkamp in the build-up. Franny Jeffers was named as a substitute but was not used. Wayne played for the whole match for the first time in a Premier League away game.

His next game was for England against Turkey in a Euro qualifying match played in front of 40,000 at the Stadium of Light. It was a vital game, as Turkey were seen as their biggest rivals. Sven was still toying with the diamond formation. England won 2–0 and Wayne was named as the Man of the Match, a performance that demanded superlatives. It was another specific moment in Wayne Rooney's life when fate seemed to propel him forwards. Determined, mature and not overawed by the occasion, he was just fearless. Ready for whatever happened to him – or as ready as you could be at that age.

Whenever he received the ball the crowd were in

anticipation and the Turkish defence seemed to back off him. He almost scored in the opening minutes when the Turkish keeper failed to gather Gerrard's up-and-under and the new England star's shot was hacked off the line. Two strong runs by him just before half-time created chances for Owen, who was not composed enough to convert them. Darius Vassell (a replacement for Owen) scored the first goal for England and Beckham scored from the penalty spot in injury time.

The next week Everton entertained Bobby Robson's Newcastle, who still had an outside chance of the Premiership title, locked in a three-way tussle with Arsenal and Manchester United. The media circus was now parked outside Wayne's house and was following his every movement, pretty much apropos of nothing. Their omnipresence is still there to this very day. Wayne was now in tremendous form, perhaps the greatest of his early Everton career. At that point he had the ambition and the strength. He commenced the match like an express train, getting straight down to business. In the first thirty seconds he burst through and really should have scored but Shay Given blocked his shot. Furious at missing a golden chance, he was relieved to see that the linesman was flagging for offside.

In an explosive opening spell Newcastle came straight down the field and Kieron Dyer appeared to have sound claims for a penalty dismissed. The Newcastle midfielder had been chopped down by David Weir but the referee waved 'play on'. When Wayne went off in the last minute of the Turkey game (to a standing ovation, I might add), Kieron had replaced him. Dyer was another player that should have been an England regular, but several coaches casually wrote off his obvious talent. After retiring he was later to write a book describing the gambling culture that was endemic in the England camp at that time. Wayne just could not be kept out of the picture. He blazed in another shot that struck Jonathan Woodgate on the arm. Another penalty claim was dismissed though, to his obvious disgust. Then he scored, Weir flicked Tommy Gravesen's shot on and Wayne, reacting quickest, headed the ball home. The goal rattled Newcastle and they struggled to control the midfield as Wayne hijacked proceedings. That swagger was now becoming part of his game. Newcastle equalised with a great goal from Laurent Robert just on half-time, which set things up nicely for the second half.

The only goal scored was the controversial penalty by Rhino, which won Everton three vital points and severely damaged Newcastle's title hopes. Thomas Gravesen's atrocious challenge on Oliver Bernard went unchallenged and Everton broke away. The quick-fire move ended with a dubious penalty being awarded. Everton went above Liverpool in the table four points behind fourth-placed Chelsea. In their next match Newcastle were butchered 6–2 at home by United and their chance of the Premier League, then known as the FA, Barclaycard Premiership for sponsorship reasons, evaporated.

Why was Wayne so good at that age? Colin Harvey knew at twelve years of age that Rooney was going all the way. One reason was that the youngster had a perspective on football details that was unmatched. The players that were at Goodison in his early days included talents like the egocentric Gazza, the balletically skilled David Ginola, Tommy Gravesen (good enough to play for Real Madrid) and of course his pal Ferguson. Like a sponge he absorbed and paid careful attention to what they did. They were the best guys to learn from, and learn he did.

David Moyes was also learning as he went along, and the players were unhappy around the start of the year because they claimed that he was working them too hard. On the morning of the third round FA Cup defeat at Shrewsbury he had them training on the Gay-Meadow pitch to accustom them to the mud-heap that it resembled. This had backfired though, as Wayne and his chums were leg-weary and fatigued. As Oscar Wilde once concluded, 'Experience was the name men gave to their mistakes.'

Everton lost to Gérard Houllier's Liverpool in their next home game, going narrowly down 1–2. Wayne was involved in the early action, clattering into the Liverpool keeper Jerzy Dudek as they both went for Lee Carsley's long ball into the box. The ball broke for Kevin Campbell, whose attempt was cleared of the line by Jamie Carragher. Wayne was everywhere, or so it seemed. He knocked the Croatian, Bišćan, in the back early on and the Liverpool defender went off after eight minutes. Michael Owen put Liverpool ahead on the half hour with a shot that Richard Wright should have saved.

It was his first goal against the Toffees in open play. In nine previous Mersey derbies he had only previously scored from penalties. Rhino equalised from the penalty spot after fifty-seven minutes when Carragher had upended Gary Naysmith. Six minutes later though, Danny Murphy won the game for Liverpool when Carsley failed to close him down and the midfielder beat Wright from twenty-five yards.

The game turned nasty. Gerrard and Dietmar Hamann had already picked up yellow cards and in the closing minutes both Naysmith and David Weir were dismissed for receiving their second yellow cards. Boy, boys, boys... Everton finished with nine men. In the second half, Wayne was later accused of spitting on the pitch in front of the Liverpool fans in the Lower Bullens Road, but nothing came of it.

Worse was to follow when on Easter Monday Everton's bogey side Chelsea beat them for the third time that season. The Toffees went down 4–1 at Stamford Bridge, the same score line as in the Worthington Cup. Wayne continued up front but was heavily marked by the Chelsea back four, which included the legend that was Marcel Desailly and the quicksilver William Gallas. Claudio Ranieri's team were 3–0 up within an hour, constantly puncturing the Everton midfield.

Eidur Gudjohnsen put them ahead after David Weir had lost his footing and just after half-time Hasselbaink headed in the second goal. Richard Wright injured himself after colliding with a post and for a while it looked as if Wayne might have had to deputise in goal for him. Steven Gerrard's cousin Anthony was on the bench but his services were not required. Wright recovered from the knock but was unable to stop the flying Jesper Gronkjaer scoring a neat third for the West London side.

Wayne contributed to Everton's consolation goal, bundled home by Lee Carsley, drifting wide and losing his markers. However, it was Gianfranco Zola who had the last word, in one of his farewell Chelsea performances. Coming on for Hasselbaink with ten minutes left, he scored what was to be his last ever goal for Chelsea with an incredible lobbed shot. The Chelsea crowd had crafted that song for him – a pastiche of the Ray Davies sixties hit by The Kinks, called 'Lola'.. You know you've finally made it when they start making up songs about you.

'La La La La Zola.' Zola, the little genius from Sardinia, retired soon afterwards, as a true legend in the game. He had been mentored by Maradona in his early days at Napoli, and the great man used to stay behind with Zola after training and teach him free-kicks. Diego loved seeing young players who had all the skills coming together.

As they left the field Zola still found time to shake the hand of Wayne, the young Evertonian. Both men were united in their passion for their chosen profession. One was at the end of his career whilst the other was just starting and learning how to handle the pressure. Wayne was still working all the time on his game, improving his technique and building his strength. Although he was nominated for the PFA Young Player of the Year, Wayne lost out to Newcastle United's Jermaine Jenas, a protégé of Bobby Robson. The decision seems incredible now looking back, but Jenas, the baby-faced midfielder, was a safe option compared to the militant gum-chewing boy from Crocky. Jermaine is now carving out a career for himself as a pundit of some gravitas and towing the party line.

The last goal scored by Wayne in his amazing debut season was the winner against Aston Villa in Everton's penultimate home game. It was his sixth Premier League goal (plus the deuce at Wrexham), and five of them had proved to be match winners. Fifteen priceless points. A feature of the costly defeats against Liverpool and Chelsea was Everton's persistent blunt tactic of launching the ball forward into the box. Mindless, route-one stuff against well-drilled, uncompromising defenders. Big Dunc had come on in the closing stages of both games in a valiant but ultimately vain attempt to unleash mayhem and salvage something. It did not change much against the Villa, except when Wayne had the ball on the deck. Once again, he was the inspiration and mainspring, fighting a tireless battle against the Midlander's defence.

In the fifth minute Wayne was put clean through by Tommy Gravesen with only the Villa goalkeeper, Peter Enckelman, to beat, but for once the youngster shot wide. For the rest of the match he was an irresistible force in the game, setting up chances with his ceaseless running. On the quarter hour he sent over an inch-perfect cross to give Steve Watson a great chance but he blazed wide. Only a couple of fine saves from Enckelman denied Wayne and Campbell as they poured down on the Villa goal.

Against the run of play Villa took the lead early in the second half. A misplaced clearance was returned to the box and their midfielder, Allbäck, headed home from close range. Moyes reacted by replacing Rhino with Duncan Ferguson, a throwback to the old days. Within minutes Everton were level, and just the presence of the ex-Rangers striker lifted the spirits of both the crowd and the team. The move was simple: a short corner on the right was played to Naysmith, who instantly crossed for Campbell to score with a perfect header.

Kevin Campbell was last seen on Channel 5, commentating on the Europa League games, wearing a neon pink shiny bow tie. Yes, honestly, he was. It appeared to be tied too tight and he seemed to be having difficulty breathing.

Wayne dropped deeper as the focal point of the attack changed. For one golden moment it looked like the Ferguson/Rooney partnership would produce a goal. Big Dunc, looking like Frankenstein's monster in a blue shirt, side-footed in a shot, Enckelman made a great save and the ball bounced out to Wayne. He slammed it straight back but a Villa defender appeared from nowhere to block the effort. Then Campbell set up the troublesome Ferguson for another chance but Enckelman managed to smother the shot. Paul Hayward, the ace football writer, once described Duncan as a 'Scottish Dirty Harry'.

This was after Ferguson hit a burglar with a vodka bottle and broke the man's jaw. If it was possible to make the Gwladys Street End's day then Ferguson did when he jabbed his elbow into the face of Thomas Hitzlsperger. This German International had won fifty-two caps and had spent a brief spell at Everton before retiring through injury.

Thomas subsequently came out as gay, the highest-profile player to speak about his homosexuality.

Under Moyes's management Ferguson was sent off four times. Five if you want to add the three-match retrospective ban he served for the following incident. Breaking into the penalty box on the right as the ball broke to the left side, Ferguson's elbow was missed by referee Graham Poll, but was picked up by the FA video panel.

The match looked to be heading for a draw when Everton won a free kick in their own half in stoppage time. The penalty area was packed with players when Stubbs sent in a long-range kick. The ball was half-cleared by Dion Dublin and fell to Rooney, who hit home a wonderful drive from twenty-five yards: a great strike which caused absolute bedlam with comic undertones, as well as effervescent celebrations amongst the Evertonians. Once again Wayne had demonstrated the sign of a natural striker who instinctively knew where the goal was and how to find it.

It would have been nice to report that the goal was the one that clinched a UEFA place but it was not to be. Despite the tremendous impact made by Wayne, Everton finished the 2002/03 campaign in seventh spot. It was all smoke and mirrors, tough to take, with the club having occupied a slot for Europe until the final day of the season. Everton lost their last two fixtures against Fulham, played at QPR's ground, and had a vital home match against Manchester United.

Sir Alex Ferguson's side were already champions with Arsenal five points behind. Beckham and Van Nistelrooy scored the goals in a 2–1 victory. Campbell had put Everton ahead, early on. Wayne had another fine game and only a great save by Roy Carroll denied him another goal. Sir Alex had taken special note of Wayne Rooney's performance against them and was making no secret of the fact that he was a great admirer of this megastar of tomorrow.

CHAPTER 21

FAKE NEWS

'I think he is really dudey.'
JOSHUA BROWNHILL WARRINGTON

JANUARY 2018

We start this chapter with an ode to Wayne by Bristol City midfielder Josh Brownhill. Born in Warrington, he was an academy player at Manchester United until 2012. Whilst there he rubbed shoulders with Wayne, who was his boyhood hero. Josh subsequently joined Bristol City and had starred in City's win over José Mourinho's Manchester United in the Carabao Cup. The press had latched onto his admiration for Rooney and published the ode quoted above, which was written by Josh when he was just eleven years old. The influence of Wayne on a whole generation of young footballers cannot be underestimated.

Meanwhile, he continued to plod on for Everton.

WAYNE ROONEY

Tottenham away was the next fixture in 2018. This year in the Chinest zodiac is referred to as 'The Year of the Dog', or more correctly as an 'Earth Dog Year'. So perhaps it was going to be a good year for the player who was nicknamed 'dog'. Tottenham were playing at Wembley that season whilst their new ground was being built. Wayne was in the side alongside the new signing, Cenk Tosun, who had been acquired from Beşiktaş for £27 million (30 million Euros). Tosun was the long overdue replacement for Lukaku, another purchase made on the watch of the Director of Football, Steve Walsh. The best thing Walsh could have done for his most talented footballer (Rooney) was to give him another good footballer to play with. A lone ranger striker like Sun, in a counter-attacking team like Everton, needed to be a savvy operator. Just how savvy remains to be seen.

Back at Wembley, for the first time in a long while Wayne had the ball in the Tottenham net early in the game. Sadly, it was ruled out for offside. Another Wembley goal would have had been a welcome addition to his collection.

That was the high-spot of the game for Wayne as Spurs went on to score four times without reply against a very average Everton. Sun, the South Korean with the geometric haircut, put Spurs in front after twenty-five minutes, side-footing home from the edge of the six-yard box. Then Harry Kane scored twice early in the second half to put the game beyond Everton's reach. We discussed earlier how Duncan Ferguson, the original Scots warrior, must have felt as he watched the emergence of Rooney at Everton whilst his star slowly dimmed. Now you could say Wayne was handing over the mantle of the bionic samurai to Harry Kane. Wayne was eclipsed that night in the latest head-to-head duel between the top gunslingers of the Premier. Kane had improved in every area of his game; he was more of a marauder of a striker, foraging up front, than Rooney was. Wayne at his peak was better coming deep, driving at goal. From that position he could always find a meticulous killer pass or put in a dribble.

The media was just wild about Harry, as he passed twenty goals in all competitions in each of his last four campaigns in the white shirt with the cockerel badge: the first Tottenham player to have done so since James Peter Greaves.

His manager, Mauricio Pochettino, a connoisseur of his striker's goals, believed that Kane was Tottenham's Lionel Messi and there is no doubt that he was their best player. Already synonyms like 'role model' and 'nice guy' were being used about him in a world where fame came in at oblique angles. Like Wayne before him, Harry had climbed the greasy pole to a world of Bentley Bentaygas, Prada overcoats, and enormous seven-bedroomed mansions surrounded by landscaped gardens.

The problem for Harry is that the shadow of Rooney's exploits and stats will always be there, just as the shadow of the Bobby Charlton's World Cup-winning side was the legacy Rooney struggled to overcome. To give Rooney, and in turn Kane's, careers coherence and purpose they must make more impressive strides towards the kleptocratic elite of English football. There is, however, always the same question, which is: who owns the future?

Kane had six goals in his last three games against the Toffees. Cristian Eriksen, another player in magnificent form that season, wrapped it up for Spurs near the end, Son Heung-min touching the ball on to Dele Alli, whose back-flick was fired home by the Tottenham ace. Wayne did his best to staunch the flow of blue blood, firing a good shot over the bar just after Spurs' third goal. Later, a superb flick by him put in Calvert-Lewin for a chance that was blocked. The stats were bad yet again though, for it was the nineteenth game in the Premier that Sam Allardyce had lost in which he had been beaten by four goals or more.

The only consolation Everton could extract from the game was when the Tottenham crowd awarded Lennon a marvellous round of applause when he was introduced into the match for Yannick Bolasie. Lennon had spent ten years at Tottenham, playing 266 games for them before joining Everton.

In the following week a strange story emerged, asserting that Farhad Moshiri had claimed that Romelu Lukaku had quit Everton after getting a 'voodoo message', inferring there was some deep parable about the rampant capitalism of the modern game. Everton failed in their bid to sign the striker's younger brother Jordan from Lazio. The Belgian striker denied the claims and said he was seeking legal advice over them.

One transfer that did go through was Chelsea's purchase of Ross Barkley for £15 million. Seeing Ross depart from his boyhood club was very upsetting for Farhad Moshiri, who told the *Metro*: 'That was the most painful, for six months, we could not find his agent. We live in a world where young men start with an agent that become their parent. They dominate the brain.'

Barkley had not featured for Everton for all season. When Sam Allardyce took over he stated that the club were resigned to losing Ross before he had got there. One of the reasons why Rooney had joined Everton was to help the young players at the club develop. He was particularly looking forward to working with Ross Barkley, arguably the player who was nearest to him in potential. In his talkSPORT interview with Alan Brazil he talked about Ross. Here are some quotes: 'He did not come from the same part of Liverpool as me … He was a massive player for us, one of the best that I have seen … I feel I can help him.'

Unfortunately, Wayne never had the chance to develop Barkley's career. Questions had to be asked about Barkley's long-term fitness and durability. Antonio Conte favoured the 3–5–2 formation which would have suited Barkley, but he was unable to break into the Chelsea team following his transfer. What's more, Chelsea and Conte were in a firestorm of scathing reviews at that time for their poor performances.

Everton made another major transfer with Sam's second signing of the January transfer window when they purchased twenty-eight-year-old Theo Walcott from Arsenal for £20 million. Theo moved after a chat with his pal Wayne, who convinced him that the move to Everton would rejuvenate his stalled career. Walcott had a long-standing friendship with Rooney, formed when they bonded in the

England squad. The first time the pair had met was back in 2006 at The Lowry Hotel in Manchester when the England team had assembled. This was before some friendly matches prior to flying off for the FIFA World Cup in Germany. Theo was now the 'New Kid on the Block', an untried seventeen-year-old who had been surprisingly called into the squad by Sven Göran-Eriksson after just thirteen appearances in the top flight.

Wayne had always been the youngest in the squad since he won his first cap three years earlier. Aaron Lennon had also been called up to the club at that time after joining Tottenham from Leeds. Flash forward to the start of 2018 and Lennon was about to leave Goodison Park to join Burnley as Allardyce cleaned house. Walcott was a huge admirer of Wayne Rooney, both as a player and a human being. In his autobiography, the aptly named *Theo: Growing Up Fast*, he gushed about his new England teammate, saying that: 'Wazza's a one-off, a sublime player and a real presence. His skill is obvious. His reading of the game is brilliant. He is one of football's great talents. The other thing about him is that he always wants to win. Always. Whatever he is doing.'

Theo was capped forty-seven times for his country. The high spot was when he scored a hat-trick against Croatia away in a World Cup qualifier in September 2008. Wayne was the provider of all three goals and Theo described him in his book as 'a joy to play with'.

Walcott became the youngest player in history to score a hat-trick for England and the first to score one for

England since Michael Owen playing against Germany in 2001. He was hoping that the move to Everton would help him force his way back into the England squad for the upcoming World Cup Finals. In 397 games for Arsenal he had scored 108 goals. Allardyce put him straight into the side for the forthcoming home game against West Bromwich. Wayne dropped down to the bench. He could only function on nostalgia for a brief period and needed to conserve his energy.

The game was marred by a horrific injury to the Toffees' midfielder James McCarthy, who suffered a double break of his right leg after a bone-crunching collision with the West Bromwich striker Rondón. After the match Big Sam confirmed that his player had fractured both his fibula and tibia. The big striker, Rondón, was so distressed by the extent of the injury he started crying at the sight of it. He had helped put West Bromwich in front after seven minutes when he set up Jay Rodriguez to score. Wayne came on for the unfortunate McCarthy, visibly upset by his teammate's accident.

Everton did not manage a shot on target at Wembley in their dismal display against their bête noires Tottenham, a point that was observed by Spurs boss Mauricio Pochettino on their website: 'It's always difficult against a team like Everton, they have a lot of good players and to not concede one shot on target against them is a massive credit to everyone.'

The Evertonians had to wait until almost half-time in the West Bromwich game before they mustered a shot on target for the first time in 2018. Jonjoe Kenny let fly from twenty-five yards but keeper Ben Foster dealt with it easily. Ironic cheers bounced around the ground at the feeble attempt and the fact that at long last they had managed a shot on target.

With twenty minutes left the ex-England combo of Rooney/Walcott combined to save a point for the Toffees. Wayne sent in a perfect cross and Theo jumped to nod down for Niasse to fire home and level the game. It was a brilliantly worked goal by the two friends. Niasse had replaced Tosun, who looked lost and badly off the pace. It was the only flash of decent football produced by Everton in the game. Against a cadre of badass defenders such as Johnny Evans and Craig Dawson they looked devoid of any inspiration and were unable to crank up their game any further to go on and win the points. But ditching Wayne from the starting eleven, or at least reassigning him to a deeper midfield role was perceived to be a weakness by Allardyce in the eyes of some fans. Unquestionably, Rooney's stamina was fading but as we have seen from his part in Everton's equalising goal, he was still capable of turning a game with his unique talent and vast experience.

Joey Barton was covering the match for talkSPORT and was sceptical of Allardyce's tactics, stating that, 'Everton fans will not put up with this style of football.'

It was a poor result, considering that West Bromwich had not won in the League in twenty attempts. Mike Parry, Joey's colleague at talkSPORT, carried on raising questions about the choice of Allardyce in his talk show the following evening. Some Everton fans were on the phone-ins, calling Sam 'yesterday's man' and expressing their disappointment that a season that at one time had promised so much was now to all intents and purposes effectively over. The lethargic Schneiderlin had been singled out by the home fans as being the poster boy for their car crash of a season. The fans were looking for scapegoats and someone to take it out on.

'Fake News' was the buzzword the year that Rooney returned to Everton, and there were incredible tales flooding Twitter and Facebook, racking up millions of searches on Google for groundless promises. Whole industries sprouted up whilst tech experts admitted the damage that fake news could do in endangering a brand's credibility. The main reason behind creating false news was ideological and, to a lesser extent, financial.

The fake news concerning Everton was that they would be a force in the Premier with a real chance of lifting some silverware, or at the very least participating in European competition on a regular basis. After a poor start, Allardyce had parachuted in, steadied the ship, but as the long, cold winter of 2017/18 wore on, it became increasingly apparent that the vast amount of money invested by Everton had not been spent wisely.

Leicester visited Everton a few nights later, which happened to be transfer deadline day. The scheduling of this had annoyed Allardyce, who told talkSPORT: 'Suppose a player I had picked for the Leicester game was the subject of transfer speculation? How would that affect the player?'

Theo Walcott scored both of Everton's goals in a narrow

2–1 victory. Wayne was in the starting line-up that night against the side that two seasons before had stunned the football world by taking the Premier League title. Following the coup d'état against Claudio Ranieri, they were not the same irresistible force but were still a useful side. Steve Walsh had been the savant credited with discovering N'Golo Kanté and Riyad Mahrez, but some of his purchases for Everton seemed unspecifiably perplexing. Walcott put Everton in front after twenty-five minutes when he steered in Sigurdsson's neat cross. Wayne assisted with Theo's second one six minutes before the break, with a steeply driven, lofted ball in the box that was headed on by Michael Keane to Theo, who volleyed it home.

The ex-Arsenal man had talked in the press about what a great history Everton had, their passionate fans, and how tough he used to find it playing at Goodison Park. Winning trophies with Everton in the future was his ambition, but to me it sounded like wishful thinking. After a bright start Wayne, looking increasingly ponderous, faded as the Leicester midfield muffled him. He was also responsible for conceding the penalty kick, which put Leicester back into the game. The penalty was awarded when Rooney held back Wilfred Ndidi with an obtuse challenge. Jamie Vardy equalised with a perfect demonstration of how to take a penalty, that is to say, like an assassin in a kung-fu movie. I wonder if such a thing as a minus assist could be introduced for every time a discombobulated player had conceded a penalty, or had made a gross error that had led to the opposition scoring.

FAKE NEWS

After dominating the first half a lazy and disinterested Everton went to pieces as Leicester frantically chased the game. They should have shared the points as Kelechi Iheanacho, their big-money signing from Manchester City, hit the woodwork twice when he should have scored from good positions. Nine minutes from time Rooney was replaced by Schneiderlin, to the disapproval of the crowd. Wayne had failed to score in six games against Leicester and had some professional ennui with the Foxes. The last time he had netted against them was in his first spell at Everton, when he had scored in a 1–1 draw at the Walker Stadium in March 2004.

His whole career had been a struggle. People said that a boy from Crocky would never make anything of himself and get a career in the Premier League. Later, they said he would not hold onto a regular place in the England team, not because of where he was from but because of the balance between his passion and judgement. The indestructible one had proved them wrong on both counts then, but now he was facing a further crisis. Could he cut it on his return to Everton? The numinous timing of his return had elated many Evertonians but in the weeks following Christmas some were asking if Wayne seemed set on going down the path of self-parody.

Things were to get worse before they got better. Sam has decided now that Wayne and Sigurdsson could not play together. As he explained to the *Metro*: 'You have to be able to cover the ground. I think Rooney and Gylfi playing together are very shrewd, very clever and talented but in actual terms of covering the ground it is difficult – it's not their strength.'

It was 'sad but true' as Dion used to sing in that wonderful old hit 'Runaround Sue'.

Neither Wayne or Gylfi Sigurdsson figured in the game at Arsenal which ended in another bad beating for Everton, 5–1. The stats made for grim reading – the Toffees were winless in twelve matches that season against teams above them in the table (drawing three and losing nine). They had won one of the last twenty-one away games. Whilst on the subject of stats it was Sam Allardyce's 500th Premier League game as a manager. It was also the day that the 10,000th Premier Game was played. Some number cruncher had even divided the games up and constructed a league table of the combat zone and Everton had crashed the top six (at number six).

Their stats were:

PLAYED	WON	DRAWN	LOST	POINTS
987	357	284	346	1,335

It's interesting to note that the five above them (in finishing order) were the dynasties of Manchester United, Arsenal, Chelsea, Liverpool and Spurs. (No Manchester City then.)

The match was a personal triumph for the Armenian ace Henrikh Mkhitaryan, who had three assists in the demolition of Everton; in fact his game was more about assists than goals. Henrikh had joined Arsenal in a straight swap deal for Alexis Sánchez, who made the reverse journey to Old Trafford. José Mourinho had purchased the twenty-eight-year-old for United from Borussia Dortmund to replace Wayne as he slowly phased him out of the Theatre of Dreams. Rooney's influence slowly dwindled but Mkhitaryan, Bundesliga Player of the Year in 2016, was never able to successfully replace him. Mourinho wanted an improvement in his physique and this emphasised just how hard Wayne was to replace, and also what a strong player he had been in his prime. Wenger's job now was to repair Mkhitaryan's confidence and restore him to being a world-class player.

Arsenal raced into a 3–0 lead in the first twenty minutes as they napalmed the Everton defence. Loan signing Eliaquim Mangala, on loan from Manchester City, must have wondered what was happening. Our friend Joey Barton was watching the match with, you would have to say distaste, for talkSPORT, and was horrified by the poor start Wayne's team had made to the game, commenting that: 'I am an Evertonian and am embarrassed by this. They are all over the joint. They are like eleven blue crisp packets floating around the pitch.'

The other new recruit for Arsenal was the £60-million record signing, Gabon striker Pierre-Emerick Aubameyang, who scored the fourth goal from clearly an off-side position. The Everton substitute Dominic Calvert-Lewin scored Everton's consolation goal with a header twenty-five minutes from the end. Everton had the best stats in the League for fighting back from losing positions, but any hopes of retrieving anything from the game were crushed when Ramsey completed his hat-trick for Arsenal.

Allardyce was cranked up to an eleven at the end of the match and was visibly furious at his team. He did not mince his words when he told *The Sun*:

> The whole team played C---p. I think they know that. I have a lot of trouble with the players taking on to the pitch what we asked them to do. So, let us write this season off as quickly as we can by staying in the Premier and then sort it out for the start of next season.

It was early February and already the season was being written off.

CHAPTER 22

WAYNE LOSES HIS RELIGION

'A talent like Wayne's comes along once in a lifetime.
We are only concerned at his progress in the blue shirt of
Everton. He is a blue and wants to remain a blue.'
BILL KENWRIGHT

EARLY AUTUMN 2003

Season 2003/04 was Wayne's second and last season at Everton in his first spell at the club. The previous season he had played a huge part in lifting the Toffees to seventh spot and the expectations were even greater for the coming one. For over fifteen years Everton had been in gradual decline but their home-grown wunderkind was seen now as the spearhead of a blue revival. The boy from Crocky, an overnight sensation of a footballer, was selling more club shirts than the rest of the Toffees put together. He was bestriding Goodison Park like a crew-cut King Kong, extravagantly fit and magnificently talented. The problems were mounting for his boyhood team, though.

Football was also changing. Chelsea had edged into a Champions League place on the last day of the season and in that long hot summer of 2003 the oligarch Roman Arkadyevich Abramovich purchased the club. A new regime was born when he walked into The Dorchester and signed the deal. Whether or not he would have taken over if the club had not been in Europe is questionable. On such matters the whole history of the game hinged, and it could be argued that the business aspects of football had sparked a Russian money revolution.

Not since deregulation and technology brought Sky into the picture has the very essence of the game been so altered. A dramatic and unprecedented spree of player-buying followed Mr Abramovich's acquisition of Chelsea as the club cast their net over the biggest names in Europe. One of their potential targets was rumoured to be the young Boy Wonder at Everton Football Club, the one who was tipped to be the shining light of English football. Acquiring Wayne looked like a marriage made in heaven. What's more, a swoop for Rooney would deprive the Toffees of their most popular player.

The Everton fans were already showing concern that they would be unable to hold onto their prime asset after his vibrant success the previous season, but it was his place in their hearts that was truly impossible to replicate. In emotional terms Wayne was priceless. There would have been an angry backlash if he was sold at any time in the near future. This would have come not only from the fans, but also from David Moyes, who had been assured by Bill Kenwright when he joined the club that he would not sell any players. Wayne's friend and colleague, Alan Stubbs, feared the worst and told *Faith of Our Families: Everton FC, an Oral History*: 'Wayne was going to go from Everton, whenever it was going to be. We knew it was inevitable. We just came to the conclusion that we wanted to enjoy him as much as we could while we had him.'

Rooney had twisted his ankle in a pre-season friendly against Rangers at Ibrox. The injury cost him three weeks of crucial pre-season training. He came on late at the old Highbury Stadium as substitute in Everton's first Premier match but was unable to avoid them going down 1–2. Arsenal finished the season as worthy champions.

Rooney's first goal of the season came in an entertaining 2–2 draw against Charlton in a midweek game at the Valley. It was his first full game following his recent injury. Charlton had gone in front with the first of two penalties from Jason Euell. Rhino conceded the penalty when he brought down Charlton's best player, Scott Parker, who spent the match doing a passable impression of a niggly Robbie Savage. Everton quickly equalised when Steve Watson hooked in a clever pass from Mark Pembridge. Joseph Yobo gave away another penalty early in the second half and Euell sent Richard Wright the wrong way for the second time.

That looked like the end of the excitement. Wayne was continuing a steady if unspectacular return when, with less than twenty minutes left, he suddenly exploded into action.

Watched by Sven-Göran Eriksson, he latched onto an innocuous cross from Gary Naysmith and in one movement turned Mark Fish and belted home a left-footer that very nearly burst the net. Rooney apologists lucky enough to behold the strike claim that it was the hardest shot ever struck in his fledgling career in blue.

Liverpool visited Goodison the following Saturday for a lunchtime kick-off. They cruised to a 3–0 victory to make it four consecutive wins at Everton. On the day the Reds showed more flair and aggression than is usual under Gérard Houllier. Everton started brightly and Wayne created two shooting chances for Radzinski with clever lay-offs. However, both chances were spurned. Michael Owen fired Liverpool ahead after some neat footwork by Harry Kewell. Wayne almost equalised immediately afterwards, following a neat exchange of passes with Steve Watson. For once his footwork let him down though and he could not dig the ball out to flash in a shot.

Owen scored again early in the second half to sink Everton's hopes of a comeback. Baroš effortlessly forced his way past Yobo to set up a tap-in for the England striker. Dudek was then called into action, saving Rooney's point-blank range header. With twenty minutes left Moyes gambled by pitching on Ferguson to link up with Rooney. A tremendous free kick by the big man left the crowd gasping as the ball crashed against the crossbar and then dropped down to bounce in front of the goal line. A goal then would have rejuvenated the Toffees and set them up for a late onslaught.

Instead it was Liverpool who scored a third, Owen

turning provider this time, for Kewell to head home. Wayne's frustrations were boiling over and in the eighty-second minute he received a yellow card for a foul and using abusive language. It was a disappointing performance by the home side who, for long periods of the derby, looked like the away team. Evertonians had lost the gloating rights over their bitterest rivals. The most telling features of the game were that Everton lacked a linking player to bring Wayne into the match coupled with their chronic defensive instabilities.

Newcastle were the next visitors to Goodison and the game ended in a 2–2 draw. Wayne only lasted half an hour, having to leave the field after Newcastle's Bernard had raked his foot down the back of Rooney's ankle. Bernard was not even booked for his challenge. Big Ron Atkinson used to refer to such crunching introductory tackles as 'reducers'. Wayne bravely tried to continue but was eventually replaced by another prodigal by the name of Francis Jeffers, who was on loan from Arsenal. Their paths continued to cross at various times since they had invaded the culture of Everton. Francis had joined Everton two weeks before, shortly after what was to prove to be his last game for the North London side in the 2003 Community Shield. It was an inglorious exit because he had been sent off against Manchester United.

The game finished two apiece, with all the goals coming in the second half. Three of these were penalties: Alan Shearer converted two for Newcastle whilst a late penalty by Ferguson salvaged a point for the Toffees. Big Dunc had come on for Watson after sixty-five minutes and had also assisted in Everton's first goal that was smashed in by Radzinksi. It was a match for the Evertonian connoisseurs, with Rooney, Jeffers and Ferguson all making cameos. These were men who had brought a fiery glamour to the club, whose fame had blossomed and defined them. The fans always responded to them because their foibles made them individuals, endearingly human. You could also view this game as a kind of 'audition' for future *Match of the Day* shows, with Shearer, Jenas and Kevin Kilbane (making his Everton debut) all on the field at some stage.

Now, perhaps you are wondering what was happening in the lives of Wayne and Coleen in those days? In his summer hols Wayne had taken his childhood sweetheart to Miami. They stayed near the mansion where Gianni Versace had been gunned down in 1997. Later, they flew down to Mexico to stay in a rented villa. Wayne went swimming most mornings and became very sunburnt, and paparazzi followed them everywhere.

The couple became engaged in October, just a few days before Wayne played against Tottenham down in London. By the end of the year they had moved in together at a house in Formby recommended to Wayne by his teammate Alan Stubbs.

Stubbs captained Everton to their best victory of the season when they beat Leeds 4–0 at Goodison Park. Wayne started on the bench, still feeling the effects of the injury sustained against Newcastle. Watson scored a hat-trick in the match – incidentally, he was another player who should have achieved more success. By the break they were 3–0 up and

Everton brought Wayne on for Radzinski towards the end of the game. He should have made it five when he was put through on his own but fired a great chance just past the post. Everton should have kicked on from this victory but in their next match they were soundly beaten 3–0 at Tottenham.

Moyes kept Wayne on the bench as he kept faith with the team that had thrashed Leeds. Spurs had recently sacked Glenn Hoddle and David Pleat was the caretaker manager. Everton played poorly and were lucky that at half-time they only trailed to Frédéric Kanouté's long-range drive. Early in the second half Gus Poyet headed the second and shortly afterwards Wayne came on for James McFadden. Even though he spent the rest of the match charging around like a bull that the Spurs defence found hard to contain, he could make little impression.

Wayne ended up being booked in what turned into a bruising match. Robbie Keane wrapped up a miserable afternoon for Wayne when he netted the third goal. The tabloids ran a story that Real Madrid had sent a scout over to check on Rooney's progress. The new conquistadores had woken up to the fact that there were fresh goldmines to plunder, such as China and Japan. Beckham had signed for them and now they were looking for new faces to satisfy their huge fan base's desire for glamorous celebrity players. The age of the galactico was upon us. Wayne was hardly catwalk material at that time, but after he'd had a shave and donned a new Armani suit, he was ready for some photo shoots for various fashion mags.

When Wayne started working again with David Moyes in

the summer of 2013 at Old Trafford, the new United boss noticed how the ex-Everton star's communication skills had improved. Moyes told *Sportsmail*: 'When he started out with us at Everton, he just wasn't good at that. But when I arrived at Manchester United, I saw how that had changed. He went out of his way to prove it to the outside world how much he had developed in that respect.'

Suffering from a minor knee injury Wayne was out of first-team action and not training with Everton but England wanted him for a mini-tour to South Africa, and the usual old 'Club' versus 'Country' type of criticism was rife. Some fans were already saying that Wayne had played better for his country than for his club that season.

Meanwhile, Everton's season was turning out to be the biggest bomb since Nagasaki. In early November Abramovich's all-stars came to Goodison Park. The speculation about Wayne joining them had intensified and Bill Kenwright (at that time Everton's deputy chairman) dismissed reports that the England striker was set to leave the club in a £35-million move. Kenwright made this assertion in the *Metro*: 'Wayne is going nowhere, David Moyes and I sing from the same hymn sheet and we have always said any club would have to pay a king's ransom for a player like Rooney. He is part of the fabric at our football club.'

Kenwright was in a very slippery position, in a place where, to the fans, ultimately whatever choice you make is going to be wrong.

Rooney was now the most coveted player in the Premier

and one tabloid had already nicknamed him 'Roonski'. The story had gained credence when a waiter in a Yorkshire restaurant had alerted the press that Rooney's agent, Paul Stretford, had been lunching with Chelsea boss Claudio Ranieri. Claudio admitted that he was Wayne's biggest fan, comparing him to a 'panther', but Chelsea had issued repeated denials.

What is more, things were not good for Everton. They had declared a trading loss of £13 million and had debts of £30 million. Selling Rooney would have made good business sense to the number crunchers.

The stress of the debts and the increasing uncertainty concerning the future of his best player was beginning to take its toll on Moyes. It was also adding to the pressure on their working relationship, a situation that was not helped by the copious amounts of publicity Wayne was receiving.

It was National Toffee Week – honestly, Everton had not scored since their goalfest against Leeds. Wayne had only managed one goal so far in that campaign and the fans were looking to him for inspiration. After the match it also happened to be his eighteenth birthday celebration and he had hired Aintree Racecourse for the benefit of the Alder Hey Children's Hospital. Some 'C' list celebs had been invited to the lavish, splendidly catered event, soap stars from *Corrie* and *EastEnders* and members of the Busted pop band, who were big favourites of Wayne at that time.

It was significant that Rooney spent some of the time at his birthday bash at Aintree talking freely to the media for the first time. From now onwards, he and Coleen were in the front seat of the roller coaster.

Busted's music should have been played over the speakers rather than the *Z-Cars* theme when Wayne came out with his buddies for the visit of Chelsea. The Everton programme for the match even had a heartfelt message straight from Rooney, declaring: 'I am happy to be at Everton. I have only just signed my contract, so I am not interested in anything that Chelsea have to say.'

So there.

In another game, Everton should have gone ahead in the first minute. Thomas Gravesen put Radzinski in after John Terry had completely mistimed his tackle. With only Carlo Cudicini to beat, the amazed crowd watched in disbelief as the ball skimmed the post. Another even closer chance came when Alex Nyarko, the Toffees' midfielder, took a pass from Wayne and crashed an unbelievable shot against the right angle of crossbar and post. He struck it so hard it was a miracle the whole structure did not splinter and crash down. Ghanaian Alex had said that he would never play for the club again after being castigated by an Everton 'anthropoid' on the pitch at Highbury two years previously.

Rooney joined in and made two attempts at his prospective employers' goal. The second was a clever lob after Cudicini had recklessly charged from his goal. It would have been a spectacular goal if it had gone in. In the first half Wayne seemed to be everywhere, racing out to the wings to collect passes from Hibbert and then tearing around in the Chelsea box as if he intended to destroy Abramovich's empire single-handed.

The second half was just seconds old when it started in 'Groundhog Day' fashion. Terry, who had a nightmare match (earning a rating of just 4 in *The Independent*), was outpaced by Radzinski, whose shot was smothered by Cudicini. (Terry was in trouble at that time following his antics in 'The Wellington' Club.) Chelsea scored against the run of play soon after. Mutu sent Geremi marauding down the right and then headed home the skimmed return.

Mutu, the self-destructive Romanian International, was talent-driven rather than ambition led. As a striker for Chelsea he had a flamboyant talent that was matched only by his ability to squander it. Yet parallels in determination and grit could be made with Wayne as he made a relentless rise from the concrete tower block he grew up in to the Premier League via FC Arges Pitesti, Dinamo Bucuresti, Internazionale, Verona and Parma. In an interview with the *Evening Standard* he stated wistfully: 'I had it rough and tough as a child but enjoyed it all the time. I love football and want to play every day of my life. I have a very sincere relationship with the football.'

Everton deserved a point and near the end Franny Jeffers, on for Radzinski, had a great chance to equalise from Gary Naysmith's cross but skewed his header well wide. It was a horrible miss.

Sven-Göran Eriksson, who had been photographed taking tea with Abramovich, had been repeatedly linked with the Chelsea job. Players had been signed on the direct recommendation of Sven and perhaps with a view to coaching the eighteen-year-old hotshot, Rooney's name had been put forward. Could Chelsea have assimilated Wayne into football's version of the Harlem Globetrotters? One thing was certain though: he was being labelled by just about everyone in the media as the future of English football. Wayne was barely eighteen yet he was now a celebrity, living a life in code, trying to decipher what everybody actually wanted from him.

The next match at Goodison Park was against Wolverhampton Wanderers, who finished stone bottom of the Premier League that season. Wayne was dancing with wolves, or dancing past them more like. So far in the season he had been subdued but now was the time for him to up his game and start showing at a domestic level what all the fuss was about. The game was effectively over as a contest in the first twenty minutes as Everton hit two quickfire goals. After fifteen minutes, Radzinski zipped through to fire a glorious shot home from the outside of the box. It was a harder chance than the two easy chances he had squandered against Chelsea in the previous home game.

A glorious run from Rooney created the second goal three minutes later. A powerful run down the right ended with him sending over a brilliant centre and Kevin Kilbane rose to send in a towering header. Only some fine goal keeping and stubborn defending by the team in old gold shirts prevented Everton from amassing more goals. Eight minutes from the end Wayne went off to a great ovation by the Evertonians. Franny Jeffers replaced him. In *The Independent* he recounted a story about Wayne's early days:

> I watched him against Spurs in the FA Youth Cup and he scored one of the best goals I have ever seen. He hit a free kick and it came back to him. He was, like, thirty yards out. He just hit the ball like he was trying to boot it out of the stadium because he was frustrated at not getting it over the wall first time. Unbelievable. He just leathered it and it went soaring into the top corner.

Wayne's season suddenly exploded as the goals started flowing. His second goal of the season came at Portsmouth shortly before Christmas. He was on the subs bench but came on for the injured Watson after twenty-four minutes. His team was trailing to Jason Roberts's first Premier League goal created by Teddy Sheringham. On his Everton debut Rooney had clashed with Sheringham, who had then been playing for Tottenham.

The arrival of Wayne seemed to galvanise his teammates and within minutes Lee Carsley had equalised for the Toffees, tucking home Kilbane's cross. Just on half-time Wayne blasted Everton ahead after the Portsmouth keeper Pavel Srníček could only palm Gary Naysmith's cross out to him. Stationed by the far post, Rooney could not turn down this early Christmas present. He just smashed in a blistering shot. Srníček, an underrated goalie, made a great attempt to stop the effort, literally and instantly flinging himself at the ball. He got a hand to it but the shot was hit with such venom that he could not stop it fizzing into the net.

The second half was an anticlimax, and Radzinski should have grabbed the third goal after Wayne set him up. With twenty minutes left, Steve Stone, another Ronin who had ended up on the South Coast, had a slight flare-up with Rooney. It was just a case of 'handbags at dawn' really, but it was caused when Wayne rather rashly pushed the ex-England midfielder over. The referee appeared and Wayne started walking off the pitch, much to the amusement of the home crowd. It was just a piece of slapstick really, and the referee called Wayne back, insisting that he was merely booking him. It must have been a strange experience for Wayne, to have a ref saving him from further punishment.

His form had improved but Wayne was becoming increasingly frustrated and disillusioned with his current situation and as we will see in the coming months felt a diminishing sense of feeling towards his club. The glare from the spotlight was intensifying.

CHAPTER 23

MANCHESTER BY THE SEA

'What a worthless, burnt-out coward I would be called
if I would submit to you and all of your orders.'
HOMER, *THE ILIAD*

WINTER 2003/04

Wayne was having a good Christmas. He came off the bench to ensure that Everton grabbed a dramatic victory over Leicester at Goodison Park on a pitch glimmering with frost. Once again David Moyes had restricted him to the role of substitute, trying to conserve his energy over the busy holiday period. An early blow for the Toffees was the loss of Italian defender Pistone with a leg injury. Wayne's chum Tony Hibbert deputised, and shortly after the injury, Everton went ahead. It was real route-one stuff, and a huge clearance from Nigel Martyn caused confusion in the Leicester defence and Lee Carsley pounced to crack in a low drive. The Leicester keeper Ian Walker blocked the goal attempt but the ball rebounded off his defender Steve Howey and into the net. It had been an unfortunate own goal, but veteran striker Les Ferdinand equalised for the Foxes with a fine drive of laser-guided precision after a disputed free kick. It was Ferdinand's sixteenth goal against Everton in his goal-strewn career.

Leicester went ahead with almost an hour played when Jamie Scowcroft stooped to head home a simple goal. Moyes realised he had to do something to salvage the game and unleashed Rooney for James McFadden, who was now sporting a shaven head. It was a master stroke. Leicester seemed paralysed with fear since the time Everton's Number 18 took to the field. Within minutes the Toffees were level, Wayne's old partner in crime Kevin Campbell carved out a chance, and Rooney scored with a savagely hit drive from the edge of the box.

Moyes played his last card, which proved to be an ace, sending on Ferguson for the tiring Campbell with twelve minutes left. They went for the jugular, and soon Ferguson rose high to nod down for Radzinski to race through and score the winner, and on this day the winger had the speed of a Tokyo-bound bullet train. Wayne was first over to congratulate the big man for his part in the goal.

On Boxing Day Everton went to Old Trafford and this time they finished on the wrong end of another five-goal thriller. A huge crowd of 67,642 watched the match, with Bellion, Butt and Kleberson scoring for the Reds. An imbecilic Gary Neville own goal and a last-minute goal from Duncan Ferguson were the reply.

Davy Moyes had met Sir Alex Ferguson privately at the Haydock Thistle Hotel to discuss Wayne's future. The United patriarch told Moyes that he wanted to sign Rooney. Moyes told him that he was not for sale. Ferguson accepted the situation but pleaded with Moyes not to let 'Rooney go South', meaning don't let him join Chelsea. Abramovich's millions had recently enabled them to sign Arjen Robben, whom United had coveted. Now Ferguson was very concerned about the speculation surrounding the impending transfer of the Everton youngster and the media attempts to muddy the waters around his club.

On 28 December, in the 'Crimbo limbo' period, Wayne did it again. The same scenario, coming off the bench to score the winner against Birmingham. In their last four games Everton had won three and Wayne had notched vital goals in all of them. In this home match he had come on at half-time at the expense of Lee Carsley for his fiftieth club appearance. Wayne's first major contribution to the match was a precise cross to Kilbane, whose first-time shot was brilliantly tipped around the post by the Brummie goalkeeper Taylor.

The Toffees cranked up the pressure and it was no surprise when Wayne put them ahead with twenty minutes left. Once again Big Duncan had created a chance by causing mayhem in the goalmouth. Naysmith had swung over a corner and Taylor could only palm it into the path of Wayne, who instantly volleyed into the net; it was not unlike the goal he had scored at Portsmouth at the start of his hot streak. Within a minute he had another clear-cut chance from the edge of the box but Taylor denied him with another stunning save. In a lighter moment there was a break in play whilst Nyarko received treatment and Wayne indulged in some friendly banter with the travelling Birmingham fans. There is no record of the conversation but at the end of it everyone was smiling. Nyarko left Goodison at the end of the season when his work permit expired.

The game ended with Wayne in action again, sending in another fierce shot that just whistled past Taylor's far post. He had dominated the second half and earned his side a valuable three points in their fight against relegation. Wayne was winning games single-handedly at times with his fantastic ability. The problem for Everton was that with every goal he scored, the clamour around Rooney grew and the headlines became bigger.

Early 2004 saw a disappointing start for Everton. Fulham knocked them out of the FA Cup after a replay and also beat them in the Premier. Charlton also won by a solitary goal at Goodison Park and Birmingham had their revenge by winning 3–0 at St Andrews. The fans were saying that Moyes was working the players too hard and that this was impacting on their fitness levels. Tomasz Radzinski had some insightful points to make in the book *Faith of Our Families: Everton FC, an Oral History*:

> Being in the same situation with Moyes, not changing the training, the same system, maybe we got a little

bit of a repeat year, where not everybody's as sharp anymore because we knew the training already, we know what he expects of us, I think this was the biggest problem the second season.

The only time Wayne scored two goals in the Premier for Everton in his first session at the club was in a 3–3 draw away to Southampton. It was a bizarre match, with Everton 3–1 up at one stage and apparently cruising to an easy victory. Wayne started quicker than Lewis Hamilton's Mercedes at Monte Carlo. In the first minute he almost scored, bursting through to pull a shot just wide from twelve yards. Five minutes later he did score though, when he set himself up neatly for a chance, instantly sending in a searing drive that hit the Saints defender Svensson and deflected past the keeper.

After thirty-three minutes they went 2–0 up with a goal from Ferguson, a typical header from Tommy Gravesen's pinpoint cross. This was the only Premier game that both Wayne and his great chum Big Duncan managed to get onto the score sheet at the same time. It must have been a great moment for Wayne, considering the fact that Big Duncan had been his childhood hero and mentor. It should have been all over a few minutes later when, following another piece of magic, Wayne, with the alchemist's touch, carved out a golden chance for his hero, but the big man blazed over the bar from close in.

As so often happens in football, Southampton were let off the hook and this was the signal for them to claw their way back into the game. Kevin Phillips, a former Golden Boot winner with Sunderland, scored a typical opportunist goal. With his nimble skills and quick feet he was an instinctive finisher. Wayne appeared to have guaranteed success for Everton when he made it 3–1 with thirteen minutes left. It was another sweet goal, Steve Watson's measured cross being firmly driven home. Mobbed by his teammates, Wayne celebrated in front of the travelling Everton fans with an attempt at a 'crowd surf', another milestone in his career having been reached. Now he went looking for his hat-trick, and he wanted to beat Dixie Dean's record of being the youngest player to score three times in a game for the club.

Wayne's father used to recount stories of when Dixie was an apprentice fitter in the railway sheds at Wirral. Dean worked nights so he could concentrate on football in the day. With his fellow night-shift workers they held contests to liquidate rats by booting them against the wall. Dixie always won these contests for some reason, and I can never see his record of 300 League goals for one club being beaten.

Southampton refused to give up though and ex-Everton striker James Beattie, who had been deployed as a substitute, scored from a full-blast penalty, which had been conceded by the Swede Tobias Linderoth. In the last frantic few minutes Fabrice Fernandes, another substitute flung on in almost desperation, teed the ball up before smashing home the equaliser with a piledriver from a long way out. A crestfallen Wayne left the field with his head bowed, for that game with Everton's late collapse had encapsulated his season: a probable victory turned into a disappointing draw by abysmal defending. Wayne was scoring goals and creating them at one end, only to see them needlessly conceded at the other by poor defensive play.

The season was turning into an unalloyed nightmare, the dreadful collective malaise bringing them down the table. Like maggots on a mouldy apple, the press was eating away at the fabric of Everton; indeed they were seen as a club in meltdown. Almost daily Wayne was linked with this club and that, and Newcastle had made an official bid of £20 million.

Everton won for the first time in 2004 with a 2–0 victory over Aston Villa. Two late goals gave them an important victory. Ferguson wore the captain's armband and Wayne started the match alongside him. The first half was uneventful apart from when Wayne, who appeared to handle the ball, had a fine opportunity for a strike at goal but had his legs taken from underneath him. No foul was given. Just on half-time Wayne was yellow carded. Ferguson and Wayne were combining well but lacked the final ball to prise open the hard-working Villa defence.

Wayne had some long-range shots but they were comfortably dealt with by the Villa goalkeeper Thomas Sorensen. In an attempt to break the deadlock Moyes sent on Tomasz Radzinski in place of Steve Watson. Our friend Hitzlsperger had Villa's best chance but was denied by a great save from Nigel Martyn. Everton pushed up and the deadlock was finally broken thanks to Wayne, who finally found some space on the right. Instantly sending over a curling cross that lured Sorensen off his goal line, up popped Radzinski to nod the ball home. In the closing minutes the Danish midfielder Gravesen scored the second goal after more good work by the Canadian International Radzinski.

At the Walkers Stadium, Ferguson was sent off for picking up two bookings. He then went looking for Steffan Freund, with whom he had scuffled when he picked up the second booking, and he placed his hands around the man's throat. At first it looked as if he was going to throttle him, then he stormed off the field. As he made the long walk, he tore off his shirt and started abusing the baying Leicester fans. He had also ripped off his captain's armband and threw it at Rooney, who gratefully put it on.

Perhaps it was a badge of honour, a symbol, a transfer of power. Like in the heat of battle where the flagbearer falls and someone picks it up. Although he was only eighteen, Wayne was a natural leader: he had the confidence, he had the chops, he could lead by example. Calling out players almost twice his age and who had far more experience than he had never fazed him.

Yet at half-time, Moyes asked him to take off the armband, and Wayne was deeply upset. Stubbs, the senior NCO and club vice-captain, wore it in the second half instead.

But Rooney had the final word, going on to captain Manchester United, his country, and to later return to his beloved team as captain.

Wayne had scored his penultimate goal of the season in that match and an injury-time goal by future Everton striker

Marcus Bent ensured it finished 1–1. Leicester finished one place below the Toffees and were relagated.

The goal that Rooney scored against Leeds in his next away game was the last one he scored wearing blue until his winner against Stoke City in the summer of 2017, some thirteen years later. The season petered out. The only game of note, if you could call it that, was a 0–0 draw at Stamford Bridge. Everton played a tight defensive game against the side that eventually finished second in the Premier. Wayne had the best chance of the game. Joe Cole had brought down Pistone, and Gravesen's free kick bounced around the Chelsea penalty area like a pinball. Kilbane fastened onto the ball and fired in a shot which was blocked but the rebound fell invitingly to Wayne, who was just yards out. With the goal at his mercy he slammed in a low drive, but the Chelsea keeper Ambrosio somehow blocked it with his legs. Such missed opportunities make the striker look at fault but the Italian goalkeeper reacted so fast and it turned out to be a wonderful block.

Chelsea never pursued their interest in Wayne at that time for reasons that were never obvious. The order would have had to come from Abramovich, not his underlings. When Mourinho returned to Chelsea for the second time the 'Special One' had an obsession with signing Wayne Rooney. However, the owner did not share that desire. The joke amongst the Chelsea backroom staff was that Mourinho spoke to Rooney more than he spoke to his wife. In fact, in the summer of 2013 he spent hours talking on the mobile to Wayne, seducing him with offers and planning a transfer 'Down South'. Abramovich did not entertain such a deal.

WAYNE ROONEY

The tensions between José and the owner came to a head in the third match of season 2013/14, when Chelsea travelled to Old Trafford. The West London side played without a recognised centre-forward, which was Mourinho's contemptuous response to the situation. Mourinho could barely conceal his apparent jealousy at Moyes, who was then manager of United and Wayne's new boss. Mourinho wears on his left wrist a deLaCour watch valued at 20,000 Euros, which has an inscription inscribed on the sapphire crystal casing that reads: 'I am not afraid of the consequences of my decisions'.

So, the wheel spins. On the last day of the season Everton were beaten 5–1 at Manchester City. The fanzines ran stories alleging that the players had been battered because they thought Moyes deserved it. The club finished seventeenth, narrowly missing relegation and having recorded a mere nine wins in the Premier. Wayne had started in twenty-six games with eight subs appearances. He scored nine Premier goals – three more than in his first season.

Wayne went off to the Euros and came back a national treasure, scoring four goals in his first international tournament. Some judges thought England might have won it if he had not limped out of the quarter-final as England were knocked out. It was Wayne's finest tournament for England, and now he was a megastar. Brian Glanville, the doyen of football writers, wrote in his seminal history of the World Cup that Rooney was to never again play as well for England as he did that golden summer.

David Moyes is recorded in *Faith of Our Families:*

Everton FC, an Oral History as saying regarding that period: 'I remember I went out to watch him in Portugal playing in the Euros, and everybody was saying, "Wayne's meeting people on yachts with his agent Paul Stretford." And I knew Paul, and I was angry. Wayne probably at that time had nearly outgrown Everton and had to step on.'

At the end of August, he signed for Manchester United for £27 million, just four hours short of the transfer window deadline. Twenty-seven days later he scored a hat-trick for United on his debut, his first senior treble.

The Evertonians were heartbroken at the loss of their favourite son. The usual abuse followed, and would have been even worse today with the rise of social media. His house in Formby was covered in graffiti, with epithets such as 'Judas' and 'Munich 58' being examples of the sentiments. His defection from his boyhood club was seen as a ruthless pursuit of his own career. Evertonian Michael Burke recalled a slogan daubed on a wall near the ground which said: 'Wayne Rooney – he could have been a god – now he is a devil'.

POSTSCRIPT

BLUE SPARROW

'Men are like pieces of paper blown by the wind.'
Welcome to the Pleasuredome –
Frankie Goes to Hollywood

LATE WINTER 2018

We started this book with a goal: Wayne's winner against Stoke on that sunny afternoon back in August 2017. I would have liked to have finished it with a goal, but as season 2017/18 rumbled on, Everton's fortunes, like the winter, appeared to be getting worse.

After the bad beating at Arsenal, Wayne was back in the side for the home game against Crystal Palace. Captain again, he got to wear the armband and marched his troops out at the start of the game with the theme from *Z Cars* blaring out. The game had attracted more attention than it really merited because Big Sam was in trouble for some derogatory comments he had made about the Palace boss Roy Hodgson.

Wayne moved the ball around well in the first half. He could no longer cover every blade of grass as he had done in his prime but his passing was as good as ever. One wonderful crossfield ball to his buddy Theo brought warm applause from the Evertonians. Two goals early in the second half from Sigurdsson and Niasse knocked the heart out of the South London side. Wayne set up Tom Davies for the third goal, his first for Everton. He was always especially pleased when a young product from the Academy started to make an impression in the first team.

Cenk Tosun, their £27-million signing, remained on the bench and the crowd were annoyed when Sam Allardyce did not give him a chance of a run-out. There were only a few minutes left and with the home side 3–0 up, it looked like a good opportunity. Sam admitted to the *Daily Mail*: 'He is struggling with the pace. That happens to more players than it doesn't when they come in, in January. There are more who struggle than succeed.'

Surely though if you were investing £27 million in a footballer, some due diligence would have been conducted? Tosun was yet to have a shot on target in the games, though in training they said his finishing was exemplary. The step up to the Premier was a massive one. Wayne had made it seamlessly, but that was because of his exceptional talent and his burning ambition.

Rooney played at Watford the following week on a Saturday night fixture. It was not one of his better games as

Everton struggled against a tough, highly organised Watford side. Wayne spent most of the game hunting down players when they had the ball. Players like Walcott and Sigurdsson struggled with the physical side of the game against sides like that. Everton looked like holding out for a point but a late goal from the burly Deeney settled the game.

The following week Everton travelled to Turf Moor to take on Burnley. Big Sam was rotating Wayne and he came on for the last thirty minutes, replacing Davies. Selecting Rooney had become an issue with the fans, as his midfield partners were struggling for form and the defence behind him was fragile. Tosun had given Everton a first-half lead with his first goal of the season, which must have boosted his confidence. Burnley fought back to win 2–1 and Everton had now collected only 8 away-points out of the 36 available to them so far that season. A hard struggle lay ahead for them, with the pressure mounting on Allardyce.

What of our hero? What did the future hold for him? Speaking of Watford, he did play a blinder at Vicarage Road one evening. I am not talking about his performance in the 0–1 defeat but his debut as a pundit for Sky Sports. He turned up on the *Monday Night Football* show which featured the men in gold shirts against Chelsea. The whole evening went swimmingly and Wayne must have been delighted at the result: a 4–1 defeat for Antonio Conte's side. This destroyed any outside chance of them retaining their title. Gerard Deulofeu, who had a spell at Everton, crowned a brilliant home debut with a wonderful goal. On loan from Barcelona he was making an effort to make Spain's World Cup squad.

WAYNE ROONEY

If Gerard ran things on the pitch then Wayne dominated the TV studio beautifully, dressed as he was in a Boss suit with a smart tie and shirt combo, and his tie remained beautifully knotted at the throat. He was happy cracking one-liners about his fellow pundit Jamie Carragher, sat within spitting distance, as easily as he used to sell him lollipops in the Mersey derbies. At one stage he announced: 'It's probably the closest Carra has ever got to me.'

One of the TV critics described Wayne as 'A breath of fresh air.'

His breath was free of Juicy Fruit because he made it through the night without chewing once.

The only thing negative comments he drew were some derogatory cracks about his gingery hair. Indeed his hairstyle was a cross between Brody in the American TV thriller *Homeland* and Mick Hucknall, circa 1990.

So, watch out, Gary Lineker! Wayne has outscored him for England and he could well be presenting *Match of the Day* in the near future.

Everybody likes a happy ending so let me tell you about a couple of recent photographs in which Wayne was pictured, which lifted the spirits of everyone who has seen them. One had been taken at Everton's training ground and showed Wayne and Paul Gascoigne, who was looking a lot healthier than he had done in years. Gazza claimed that he had gone there to collect £40 he had given Wayne eighteen years ago. The teenage Wayne had starred in an Academy game and Gazza had slipped him the money 'for a couple of pints'. Famous for his unstinting generous deeds to the youngsters at Everton, the Geordie was calling in the debt plus compound interest!

The other picture was a heartwarming scene of Wayne with the latest member of the Rooney clan: baby Cass Mac Rooney, who weighed in at 8lb 10oz. His other sons were also in the picture: Kai (aged eight), Klay (aged four), and two-year-old Kit. Wayne signed the photo with the note saying: '5-a-side team complete'.

Watch out for them in the Everton line-up, 2035!

ACKNOWLEDGEMENTS

Firstly, I would like to thank John Blake for giving me another Firstly, I would like to thank John Blake and Rosie Virgo. Special thanks, also, to Michael 'Burkey' Burke – always a Blue – whose specialist knowledge on Everton FC and wonderful legal brain was absolutely essential to this project.

I was privileged to spend time in the company of my idol, Terry Venables, who was good enough to impart some of his vast knowledge about the art of goal scoring as personified by the likes of Greaves and Messi. This gave me a deeper understanding of just how good a player Wayne Rooney was in his pomp.

One of the first matches I attended with my twin brother Ken was Spurs vs Everton. We stood behind the goal with some of the Everton lads, who had travelled down to London to watch their idol –Alex Young, 'The Golden Vision', and that is when I first became aware of the power of the beautiful game. Without the help of Ken, I would never have made it this far.

A brief thanks for the help of the special people who watch over me in my day job: Natalie Ferer, Julian Rigby and Vic Van Rensburg.

And, of course, thanks to my wonderful family: my wife, Marie, for being there for me and my daughter, Jac. She is the mother of two little girls – Fifi and Elizabella – who are the most advanced readers in their school. God bless you all.